With Dignity and Grace

WITH DIGNITY AND GRACE

To Robin —

Best wishes —

DAPHNE WORMELL &
JULIA TURNER

Julia Turner

Past M&K.

Hinds

Published by Hinds
13 Carlisle Avenue
Dublin 4
Ireland

First published 2013

ISBN 978-1-909442-01-6

Typeset in Agmena Pro
Design by Bill Murphy Design
Printed in Ireland by W&G Baird Ltd

TABLE OF CONTENTS

Table of Illustrations   vii

Foreword   ix

Acknowledgements   xi

Preface   xiii

Part One by Daphne

  1. Beginnings 1916–22   3

  2. First Trip to Ireland 1924   11

  3. Ottawa and Fassett 1925–32   15

  4. Extracts from 'Jotty,' Daphne's First Diary 1930–32   21

  5. Return to Calgary 1932–35   33

  6. Brownstown House, County Meath 1935   37

  7. Home to Calgary 1935–37   51

  8. Undergraduate at Trinity College Dublin 1937–40   55

  9. Courtship and Marriage 1940–41   69

 10. Cambridge & Bletchley Park 1941–44   75

 11. Home at Mount Merrion 1945–49   89

Part Two by Julia

12. Donald   113
13. The Wormell Family   129
14. Nannie   133
15. Home at Gatineau from 1949   137
16. Teaching, writing and influencing   143
17. Women's Ministry in the Church of Ireland   157
18. Home to Canada 1964–2000, and Home...   177

Appendix I   Women and the Church   183
Appendix II   Elizabeth Moloney, Former President of the
              Irish Pre-School Playgroups Association   193

Index   199

TABLE OF ILLUSTRATIONS

Daphne, about 2 years old, Calgary c. 1918   93

First trip to Ireland, on the beach at Skerries, 1924   93

Wallace House, Bowness, 1916   93

A happy day at Fassett, Quebec, 1928   94

Daphne as a happy Ottawa teenager, c. 1930   94

Daphne's last winter in Ottawa, 1932   94

Daphne helping to make the hay at Brownstown House, 1935   95

Wallace Family at Calgary, 1936   95

Dublin University Elizabethan Society Officers and
  Committee, 1938–39   96

Daphne awarded Scholarship, Trinity Monday, 1939   96

Daphne taken by Donald, during their courtship, 1941   97

Don in the Wicklow hills, 1941   97

Portsalon Beach, August 1944   97

Wedding Day, December 12, 1941   98

Full wedding party with Daphne and Don, December 12, 1941   99

Daphne holding Julia, with Richard and Donald, 1947   99

Kitty (née Keating) O'Reilly with Wormell children, 1952   100

At the church for the wedding of Renée Fleury, 1953   101

Gatineau, c. 1960   101

Wormell family, 1968   102

Elizabethan Society Garden Party, Trinity Week, 1967   102

At Gatineau, in front of Don's flowers, 1977   103

Daphne giving a talk on the RTE programme 'Outlook', 1982   104

Daphne at Lennon Family Reunion, Niagara-on-the-Lake, 1983   104

Patricia Hastings-Hardy and Daphne, Canterbury Cathedral, 1986   104

Wallace House on Golden Street, Ottawa, 1987   105

Don after his retirement   106

Daphne at the wedding of Susan, Betty Cole's daughter, 1992   106

Approaching Daphne Island, Athabasca River, Alberta, 1993   107

Daphne on Daphne Island, Athabasca River, Alberta, 1993   107

Daphne in her garden, 1995   107

After conferring of Honorary Degree at TCD, 1996   108

First female Lay Readers, Diocese of Dublin and Glendalough, 1997   108

25th Anniversary of Commissioning as Lay Readers, 2000   109

Bella Napier, 'Nannie', 2000   109

Daphne and Julia at Kilmacanogue, Co. Wicklow, 2001   109

Clerical group outside Rathmichael Church   110

Members of the Women's Ministry Group Committee   110

FOREWORD

Daphne Wormell's life was so rich, and her quality contributions in various fields so many, that few who knew her could be aware of the full compass of her activities and her talents. This account will fill in many gaps for most of us, and for others it will call up happy memories of hours spent in the company of this brilliant, loving and versatile woman, who arrived from Canada to study in Trinity College Dublin at the age of twenty-one and remained in Ireland for the rest of her life.

My own memories of Daphne date from her later years, when we worked together on the Women's Ministry Group in the Church of Ireland, which she chaired. Some of these can be found in my book *Embracing Women: Making History in the Church of Ireland*[1].

One thing that was great, though somewhat deceptive, about Daphne was her gentleness, which disguised her strength and determination, as she provided leadership and support for women sensing a vocation. She was an admirable talent scout and networker, always coming up with the right person to help solve a problem, attend a special meeting, or fill a vacancy. In this, her contacts through TCD, where her husband Donald was Professor of Latin, and her committee memberships in the Church of Ireland, were invaluable; and her recruits were always willing, charmed as they were by Daphne's appeal. A major point of

---

1 *Embracing Women: Making History in the Church of Ireland*, Ginnie Kennerley, The Columba Press Dublin, 2008

agreement between us was the importance of sweet reasonableness, coupled with serious study, in making women's voices heard and women's vocations accepted in the Church. We agreed that no one would be entitled to speak of us as 'viragoes' or a 'monstrous regiment of women'.

As Daphne said to Patricia Hastings-Hardy as they processed together up the nave of Canterbury Cathedral, we should act with dignity and grace. Of course this required no special effort for Daphne; it was her natural approach to everybody!

Daphne was a remarkable woman who moved from a hard life in the prairie country of Western Canada during her childhood in the 1920s to the challenges of raising a family through the war and post-war years in England and Ireland. From the beginning of our friendship, I was aware of her warm dedication to the causes she believed in, her compassion and her lively mind. It was also clear that she was a devoted mother and grandmother, a loyal wife and an expert home-maker. But only in reading the pages that follow have I become aware of how great a contribution she made in so many areas, both personal and educational, as well as in the Church of Ireland.

I owe her much for her many personal kindnesses. She was the kind of person who could deal with great issues but never forgot the little things which make such a difference to individuals. When I had taken all four Christmas services within fourteen hours in my first year as rector of Narraghmore and Timolin with Castledermot and Kinneagh in South Kildare, and refused all local invitations to Christmas dinner to avoid offending any of my new parishioners, it was typical of Daphne to invite me to share in the festivities at her home in Shankill. She was one of my most loyal friends and encouragers. What a lot I and all the first generation of women clergy owe to her!

So it is a delightful privilege to write this Foreword to the story of Daphne's life and achievements. She came to the task of writing it as she did many others: she started, indicated the way, and then handed over the baton – in this case saying to Julia, her only daughter, 'There, Julia. We got to the Fifties. Now you know all the rest.' Of course, Julia did not know all the rest, and had to do much research to complete her mother's story. The result is a wonderful tribute to a great lady indeed.

Ginnie Kennerley,
Dalkey,
September 2013

ACKNOWLEDGEMENTS

Warmest thanks are due to many who have been a part of this project. It began as a birthday gift to Mum on her 81st birthday, 7th June 1997.

Daphne was the inspiration, her sister Val the encourager and my husband, Ralph, the supporter.

To Anstice Parke I send deep thanks for her efforts over several years in not only taping Daphne, but in also patiently asking the right questions and in striving to capture the essence of what was being said. Thanks also to Robin Wormell, who persisted in catching details of Daphne's war experiences. It was Val who took the time to tape Daphne's recollections of her experiences in the Church of Ireland.

It is a long way from Dublin to Vancouver Island, and there were difficulties with tapes being misplaced for several years. Panic is a good word! Many thanks to Stephen Wormell who spent hours making tape duplicates and so saved the day. Thanks also to David Ganly, son of Michael and Sandra Ganly mentioned in the text, for copying tapes and organising their shipping.

How fortunate it was that two friends of one of my sons were still living here in Port Alberni, British Columbia, and were available and willing to help with tape transcriptions and computerising of sermons. Karin McCaig and Myra Wright began their efforts as a duty, but quickly became very interested in Daphne's life and story-telling. Their interest was greatly encouraging. Thanks, girls!

I leaned on Ann Budd for advice, and she provided that and much, much more as time went by. Melissa Webb was always encouraging, having been involved with a similar project herself. And thanks to Ginnie Kennerley for her advice and support, and her willingness to contribute.

In the chapter 'Daphne and the Church' I freely used the words and writings of others, several times without credit, although always with permission. These people were most generous in sharing. Contributions came from Jennifer Gill, Dr Michael Kennedy, Ginnie Kennerley, Horace McKinley, Fred Appelbe, Hazel Tamplin and Patricia Hastings-Hardy.

In other areas, I am grateful to Daphne's longest surviving sibling Dorothy Short, and also to my brothers for answering endless questions. Gratitude is due to Helen Fosbery for her assistance with the 'Jotty' diary, and to Geordie Hallowes, son of Aunt Olive, who had the Murphy memory and could recall details long forgotten by the rest of us. Many thanks to Elizabeth Moloney who so willingly gave her time for interviews. Leslie Greer, Ann Budd, Rose Gwynn and Cherry Dowrick all provided quotes I could use to great effect. Thanks also to Norah Kelso of TCD for her speedy confirmation of some facts.

I am most grateful to the two poets who gave permission for their poems to be reproduced here: Muriel E. Critoph for 'Alone?' and Clarissa Pilkington for 'An Account of Some Recent Activities of the D.U.W.G.A. 1984'. Valentine Urie's poem 'To Don' is taken from the Wallace Papers and is a treasure of the Wormell and Urie families.

Special thanks go to my new friend in writing, Margaret Growcott, who knew nothing about Daphne and whose great editing skills proved invaluable. She would read a chapter and say, 'Who is this person mentioned here?' After my explanation she would tell me 'Julia, I don't know that. Your reader won't know that. They're not interpreters, you know. Fix it.' It was a huge asset having fresh views expressed, especially from a truly British girl.

It was Daphne's suggestion that I approach Ross Hinds and ask him for his help with this book. 'He's very good at it,' she said. 'And you will get along well with him.' How very wise her words were, for he has been all of that and more. I will never forget his patience and understanding.

Finally a big thank you to all my relatives, especially cousins Alison Wormell in Scotland and Jean Gundersen in New Zealand, and to my two sons Craig in Germany and Derek in Vancouver, and to all those friends on both sides of the Atlantic for their encouragement and patient queries regarding this project.

Julia Turner *née* Wormell

PREFACE

Dad loved to tell us about the name Daphne. This is what we would hear:

> Apollo was the god of all the fine arts, medicine and eloquence. His great dexterity in the management of the bow is celebrated. He attacked Python, a serpent who was persecuting his mother, and he killed it with arrows. He then had a dispute with Cupid – over the power of his darts. So Cupid made Apollo enamoured of Daphne, a daughter of a river. Daphne received with distrust and horror the addresses of the god, and fled from him. Apollo pursued her, but Daphne entreated the assistance of the gods, who changed her into a laurel. Apollo crowned his head with the leaves of the laurel, and ordered that the tree be forever sacred to his divinity.
>
> It is said that Daphne was admired by Leucippus, son of the king of Pisa, who, to be in her company, disguised his sex, and attended her in the woods, in the habit of a huntress. Leucippus gained Daphne's esteem and love; but Apollo, who was his rival, discovered the disguise when Leucippus went to bathe. Apollo had Leucippus killed.

It sounded exciting to us. We also liked the laurel bushes by the garden fence, because we would break up a few leaves, put them in a clean jam jar and then trap a butterfly or a bee. When the lid was on, the fumes from the leaves quickly sent the bug to sleep.

Not until Mum was in her eighties did it come to light that she was called 'Daphne' after a boat on which her great-uncle, her father's mother's brother, had sailed as an officer-surgeon in the Royal Navy, in the Indian Ocean. Her middle name, Dillon, was the last name of that same officer. He had died in Africa in 1873 on an expedition sent by the Royal Geographical Society to find David Livingstone, just over forty years prior to Daphne's birth, in 1916.

Daphne's father, James Wallace, was born in Dublin on 21st August, 1870, and graduated in Experimental Science in 1892 from Trinity College, Dublin. He emigrated to Canada and became a Dominion Land Surveyor, working out of Calgary, in the early 1900s. He surveyed large portions of the Alberta border. Daphne's mother, Eva Murphy, was born in Enfield, Co. Meath, on 24th May, 1886. She, too, emigrated to Calgary where she met Jim Wallace. Eva's father, with whom Eva did not get on, had been Rector of Rathcore Church, and Professor of Irish at Trinity College from 1896 to his death in 1919.

Eva and Jim were married in Calgary in 1915. They had five children: Daphne, Hugh, Dorothy, Valentine and Brian.

Daphne always felt that her father's attitude and behaviour were those of an early Victorian gentleman. He had a fear of sex, terrified that his daughters would somehow be destroyed by it, and he felt he had a duty to protect them by corralling them when they were growing up. He was particularly restrictive with Daphne, the eldest. By the time the other girls became teenagers, he had mellowed somewhat.

When Daphne was in Dublin, the Wallace family had all emigrated or died out. However, on her mother's side, the city was full of her uncles and aunts and their children. Most of them were doctors, having attended Trinity College.

It was in 1949 that we all moved to a house on Sandyford Road. One day, shortly after settling in, the phone rang. 'Mrs Wormell, this is the Post Office. You have to put a name on your house, so that you can have a proper address. We need to know this morning.' Daphne said, 'I'll consult my husband, and I'll ring back.' Don was in Trinity, and as he was giving a lecture he was unavailable. Daphne was at a loss as to what to do. All she could think of were place names in Canada from her childhood. One of her favourites was the valley of the Gatineau River, where she had spent happy family summer holidays at Fassett, in Quebec, during the years when the family had lived in Ottawa. She settled on the name 'Gatineau'. In time, various versions of this choice appeared on envelopes, the most common being 'Gateaux', a brand of cake. Difficulties arose when giving an address over the phone, as the correct spelling for 'Wormell' followed by 'Gatineau', was more than most could manage.

How fortunate that Mum lived to the good age of 85. In the summer of 2001, when I was over for a visit, we both knew that time was running out. We would go shopping hand in hand, not just because Mum was unsure of her footing, but we needed to hold onto each other. Each slow step was precious, each moment to be treasured: her chat with the butcher, her smile with the supermarket clerk, the wave over her head to a friend. At home, in 44 Seaview Park in Shankill, the walk across the road to buy the newspaper, the watering of the greenhouse flowers, and the dusting of the pieces of furniture still with her from Gatineau, all took on special significance.

Living to 85, with her vast, clear memory still intact, gave time to organise her papers, sermons, diaries and letters, and provided the opportunity for Daphne to record recollections. Her child bridesmaid, Anstice Parke, was enlisted to visit from England to ask questions that would spark reminiscences. They got as far as the 1950s. With delight, Daphne handed me the tapes, glad to have a load lifted from her shoulders.

To ensure that Daphne's voice comes through, Part One is compiled from tapes, diaries and letters, all written or spoken by her. She herself is telling her story. I added Part Two to fill in some gaps, and to convey something of the second half of her life.

Julia Turner *née* Wormell

PART ONE by Daphne

1

BEGINNINGS 1916–22

I was born on June 7, 1916, in a large house that stood alone on the wild Canadian prairie. We were out in the country, three-quarters of a mile from any other home. In the distance we could see the Rocky Mountains, and all around were the foothills. When I came to Dublin and saw where my father had been born, in Kerrymount House in Foxrock, I realised how similar our view of the foothills had been to that of the Dublin Mountains of his youth. Perhaps the similarity had been a major consideration when my parents had bought our house.

We lived in Bowness by the Bow River, outside Calgary. According to my father, the Bow River takes its name from a nearby stand of Douglas Fir trees that the plains Indians used for making bows. Our house had a wooden frame, with large rooms, but we were short of bedrooms, with seven people in our family.

I remember something from before I was two years old. I had hurt my hand very badly. I couldn't see up over the windowsill, and my mother was looking out across the prairie where we lived and she was saying, 'Well, I think that milkcar would just take us into town to the doctor.' I managed to push my chin up on the windowsill and I saw the red milkcar which collected milk from the local farmers. That is my first memory.

We didn't have a car. We lived eight miles outside Calgary, which was then a town of about 60,000, with one main street. We usually went in to town on the streetcars, which were trolleys, or electrified trams. Our house was about three-quarters of a mile beyond the end of the line. There were only two departures in the mornings, one at 8 a.m. and one at 9 a.m. Fortunately, there was the 10.30 a.m. milkcar. That is why my mother was anxious to catch the milkcar.

Our lives were governed by streetcars. We had to watch the time. We were very good runners, and were known as 'the Wallace Runners'. We got to know the conductors well. They would see us coming along the path over the open prairie, and they would wait for us.

We were very far ahead of our time, for we always had electric lights. And we had a telephone, a party line. You could tell by the number of phone rings which family was getting the call. We were one long ring and five short rings. The normal thing was that you would listen in to the conversations. One farmer used to sit under the phone on the wall in the evening, and reach up and listen in, every time the phone rang. The phone operator worked out of 'Central' in Calgary. 'Central' was very important. There was one story where a couple couldn't get a babysitter. They left the phone off the hook in the crib with the baby. If the baby started to cry, 'Central' would call up the house they were visiting and tell them they were needed at home, as the baby was crying.

It wasn't possible to phone across the Atlantic then; instead, one sent cables. One time the phone rang in the middle of the night in 1919, and my mother ran down to answer the phone, because my father was deaf and he couldn't hear. 'Central' asked, 'Could I speak to someone else on the phone because I have some bad news?' My mother replied that she was the only one, and then she was told that a cable had arrived to say that her father had died. I don't like hearing phone calls at night; it was built into me by that experience.

We had an electric cooker. There was a kitchen, and a small scullery where we kept our dishes and did our washing up. We were so many with seven in the family, we didn't have our meals in the kitchen, but in the dining room. As my father's deafness got worse and as we grew more loquacious, he found it very frustrating at meal times. It was decided that he would have his meals alone in the kitchen, where he could read while he was eating. We then felt free to joke and laugh, and to chat on and on in the dining room. So the dining room became the main room, and around that table was where most of our family life seemed to take place. We had an encyclopaedia and a dictionary nearby, and there were always arguments about words, about geography, about whatever came up. The encyclopaedia had four large volumes, and even today we all know that the first was 'A to Cre', the second was 'Cre to Imf', the third was 'Imf to P' and the last was 'P to Z'. We used the dictionary to look up words and to find out about them. We educated ourselves that way. It left us all with a huge curiosity about facts and about words.

We had no radio, so newspapers were very important. My father would bring one home every day from work. They were available from Toronto and Calgary. One time when we went out to a tea, Mother asked if they had any news. The host replied, 'Oh, no, I couldn't tell you any. I get all my news from home.' He refused to read Canadian newspapers. He waited until a paper came from back home in Ireland, and at that time it was two to three weeks for any mail to get through.

Every Canadian house has a basement. I cannot understand why it has not been taken up to some extent in this country, where there is so much damp coming up from the ground. Our furnace was down there, and it gave us a certain amount of heat. We could go down and make as much noise and mess as we liked. Calgary was lucky to have natural gas, so our furnace was on Turner Valley gas. We could turn it up and turn it down and it was cleaned out once a year. It was comparatively simple, with radiators in each room. So we had central heating, and we had to have it to get through the harsh winters.

I heard stories about some of the smaller farmhouses, in Saskatchewan in particular, hardship stories, where they just had a main stove and a big room downstairs, and upstairs the water froze in a drinking glass. Even downstairs the frost could come in along the edge of the door. In some ways I was colder when I came to Ireland than I had ever been in Canada, because of no central heating, and the coldness of the houses here. I developed bad chilblains at that time. That was my first impression of Ireland, how cold it was. People used to say to me: 'Well, you've been exposed to great cold. You must be feeling happy to be here.' I used to reply that never in my life had I been as cold as I had been since coming to Dublin.

The bedrooms in Bowness were all upstairs. My father had his study up in the loft, where he did some writing of Canadian History. We used to go up there to see him, to watch him pounding on his typewriter. But he wouldn't allow anyone to sleep up there because he was afraid of fire, worrying that we would be trapped. Fire was a very real menace. To have a house burn down wasn't as unusual as it is in Ireland where houses are not built of wood. The trouble was, in those early days, that people burned wood. Their chimney would be built up through the centre of the house from the furnace, to minimize heat loss. The chimney would become unduly hot and overheat the house's wooden frame. On a cold night it was tempting to stoke up the furnace too much, and there was grave danger. Every winter, particularly when we lived in Ottawa, we would see a house in flames. It was a gruesome sight, as we didn't know how many had managed to escape.

We had a succession of dogs, and we kept pigeons in with the hens. One winter, when a severe wind came down from the north, it was freezing up. The pigeons died, even the hens suffered, and there was no way of bringing them into the house. I remember it being 60 degrees below zero, and we were all crouched around the stove we had for heating the water. My father had to go out, but he wouldn't allow any of us out of the house. I remember that happening only once.

The 24th May was always a holiday with us:

> 24th of May is the Queen's birthday.
> If you don't give us a holiday, we'll all run away!

That was set out as a very definite holiday. The Queen, of course, was Queen Victoria. No-one gardened until 24th May, so we were late starting our garden. People would put in long hours of gardening, and once the warm weather came, accompanied by the long hours of daylight, everything grew very quickly. Some gardeners would even work at night. By September, everything was put to bed. Calgary had the chinook wind, warm and dry. It would rise up over the Rockies, drop its moisture high up on the peaks, and sweep down into Calgary's valley, sucking up the moisture. I've seen snow vanish into the air without melting first, and the temperature vary by 60 degrees in 24 hours. This was a great blessing, because it gave a break from the winter weather. Edmonton, which was 200 miles to the north, wouldn't get these winds, and it was considered a very bleak, cold place. So we boasted about our chinook. The trouble was, if you had fruit trees or other exposed plants, with the warmth their sap would start to rise, and when the winds stopped and the cold weather returned, the plants would be killed off. I gather Calgary is very tree-lined now for they have learned which trees do best there. But in my youth the town was devoid of greenery most of the time. Our house was close to the Rocky foothills where it was more sheltered, and we had more greenery.

If you went about five miles beyond our home, there were some very good farms with good soil. Many had horses; Alberta was a great province for horses. Even the Prince of Wales owned a ranch in southern Alberta. We had enough land for the grazing of a cow. The Bow River flowed very close to our house. This river was a wide mountain stream, and it went along at a tremendous pace. We couldn't put our feet into it or we would be swept away. We would throw things into the water, and watch as they shot away downstream, but that was as close as we came to the water there. There was an amusement park nearby, and water was channelled in there from the river, using a dam to create a little side creek. Our property was on the exit part of that creek, and we used to swim in there, and it was quite safe. It was very cold in the spring, with lumps of ice floating along as the water came straight down from the Rockies.

When Hugh was born in May, 1920, my mother didn't recover well from the birth. She had to give up nursing the baby. My father's sister, Aunt Jane, a trained nurse, arrived to help, but she put too much solid in the baby's bottle; she overdid it. Hugh's stomach became badly upset, and his digestive system was permanently damaged. At the same time, Aunt Jane resented my being around her in the kitchen, doing things I'd been taught by Mother to do to help out. The household had gone from a happily set out house, to all this upset.

It was about this time that a dreadful incident occurred. Dad had the habit of picking up a small stone and flinging it at the dog if the animal was being a pest. One day, I must have been doing something outside that bothered Dad, and I suddenly realised that he had bent down to pick up a stone. He lifted his arm to fling it my way. Petrified, I froze. Dad lowered his arm but something broke between us at that moment. Up to then, I had been the apple of his eye, his only child. Now I had to compete with a sick baby for attention, and, even if only for a moment, he had considered treating me like the dog. Our relationship never recovered.

I got the most awful attack of ulcers in my mouth. There must have been seventy ulcers, a very bad case of thrush. I also began to stammer, my mother saying it was the worst stammer she'd ever heard. It went on all that winter, when I was four years old. My father would get very annoyed at my stammering. Then, eleven months after Hugh was born, mother had another baby, Dorothy. She arrived in April, 1921.

At mother's urging, in July, 1921, Dad arranged for all of us to go, without him, for a holiday in Victoria, on Vancouver Island, a great travel destination for Calgarians. We stayed with a farming family, the MacGregors, who lived just above a lovely beach in Cordova Bay. My mother told them all about my stammer, and gave instructions that no matter what happened, no-one was ever to refer to it. They did exactly as she asked, and I returned to Calgary cured. I have never had a stammer since.

I wasn't sent to school until I was eight and a half, which was a terrible mistake. There were no children my age nearby. As a result, I always found it very hard to relate to other children. A girl my age came out to visit with her mother one day. I just stared at her, not knowing what to do with her, and resentful that she came at all. I used to want to be an only child, because then I would have adult conversation all the time.

My father had the idea that a child's character develops best when not being pressured. He felt the schools would steamroll a child without stimulating much 'individuality', one of his favourite words. When I read Rousseau later on, I realised my father had many similar ideas. It was very hard on my mother, who had no proper help during the long winter days. At one point, there were four little ones at home, and not enough for them to do.

My parents, like so many from the British Isles, were rather baffled by the Canadian school system, which is that you go to the nearest school, with everyone from down the street and across the railway line. Classes were large, up to forty at times. Even though they had extremely good teachers, adept at managing the large numbers, my parents weren't too keen on this idea. Across Canada, private schools educated the children of parents from the British Isles. There was no senior school for boys in Calgary. They were sent to Toronto, and felt very left out when they returned. My parents approved of St Hilda's School for Girls, the one private school for girls in Calgary.

I will always remember that Dad gave me a watch my first day of school. I'm afraid I lost that watch, but I do have another one that he gave me, later. When school started after Christmas, I was taken in to the headmistress's study by my father. It was all very pleasant, and the headmistress took me along the corridor to the classroom. She showed me where to hang up my coat. The next day Dad came with me to the gate of the school, and he said, 'Now, you can go on.' I went straight in and knocked on the headmistress's door. I had no idea it was not what one did. She was rather amused, and was good about it. I soon settled in to the school.

My mother was horrified by the cost of the uniform, and so she mixed and matched my clothes. It is a dreadful thing to do to children when they go to school. Children must have the proper clothes, or the same clothes as the other children, and I was very upset about it. And I couldn't say anything to her, as she was expecting my younger brother, her fifth child a month later, and she was a bit addled. I never did tell her how the lack of the proper school uniform had been such a difficult thing for me.

Dad used to take us for walks on Sundays. One Sunday, Mother was expecting visitors so he took me down to the Bow River. At that point, the river divided in two and an island had formed between the two parts. When the railway was put in across the river there, they had to have two bridges, one over to the island, and the other from the island across to the other side. They were called the Twin Bridges.

Dad was very anxious to explore a bit, so that Sunday he took me up on the first bridge and we started to walk along it. It was a railway bridge only, with no place for pedestrians. There were just the ties. I looked down and between the ties I could see the water flowing very fast underneath. I held onto Dad's hand tightly. Suddenly, there was a whistle, which indicated a train was coming momentarily. It was horrific. I was seven, and quite well covered. Dad wasn't a big man, was well into his fifties, and he didn't know what to do – to go forward or go back. Somehow, he took me up in his arms, heavy load that I was, and he ran back towards our starting point. I remember tumbling down the bank, only just in time before the train flew by. The horror of it is what I remember. Dad had thought up to then that he knew exactly when every train came, but this must have been an extra Sunday train.

I was at St Hilda's for two terms, followed by only one month in the autumn, as the family was about to be uprooted. At school, we had an excellent children's drama teacher. I got into a play, and it loosened me up a bit. I was painfully shy at the time; I 'wouldn't say Boo! to a goose.' But, I gather that later on in the term I became naughty, and I was due to get into a lot of trouble if we hadn't moved to Ottawa.

2

FIRST TRIP TO IRELAND 1924

When I was seven, in February 1924, my mother took me and the other three children on a trip to Ireland. My father came down to Montreal to see us off, accompanying the family on the train from Calgary. Suddenly, he started saying over and over to Mum, 'I have to talk to you.' Mum kept replying, 'I'm busy. I have to get the children to bed. Later. Later.' Finally he said, 'It's important. I have forgotten the passports.' The boat would be sailing from Montreal in a few days, so this was a crisis. Dad had some friends in the Civil Service; he phoned ahead from a train station and the friends managed to get all the passports together in time.

Dad had insisted that Mother needed help during the crossing. He had arranged for his sister, Aunt Jane, to accompany us, to help with the children. But Aunt Jane didn't help at all. She was too much of a fusspot, certain a child would fall overboard. Val, a baby at that time, nearly died on the boat. There was no refrigeration, the milk went sour and she was poisoned. Val became very ill; she had too high a fever for a baby, but she pulled through. To prevent disaster recurring on the return journey, my mother made sure to have Val on powdered milk long before we left Ireland, and Aunt Jane was not invited to re-join us on board.

Going back to when my mother, Eva, and all her siblings were young, they had developed a language of their own, down in the Irish countryside where they had grown up. One particular day they were taking turns making speeches, having climbed up on the pillars of the gate of the avenue leading to the house. There was a man who used to work for them who 'wasn't the full shilling.' They persuaded him to go down to the gate, too, and they encouraged him to take his turn up on the pillar to make a speech. Mounting the pillar and referring to my mother's sister standing across the gate on the other pillar, he said, 'Miss Olive is on the pier and she's sounding her voice exthorny!' That became a great family saying.

The purser on the Atlantic crossing came to my mother and said, 'There is a cable come for you, Mrs Wallace, but I can't understand it. It seems to be in code.' My mother looked at the cable, which said, 'Miss Olive is on the pier, and she is sounding her voice exthorny'. Mother knew at once that Olive was going to be in Liverpool to meet the boat, and Olive was indeed the first person we saw as the boat docked. We all spent that night in Liverpool, staying with a friend of the family, and then we crossed over by the morning boat to Dublin. We travelled on to Skerries, north of Dublin, where my grandmother was living at the time.

I remember mother would take me up to Dublin to go shopping. I wasn't very keen on shopping. We would get off the train at Amiens Street Station, and it would be about 10 a.m., which was the time for funeral processions down O'Connell Street and through the streets of Dublin. It was quite an industry. A long line of black horses with black plumes, all pulling the hearse, followed by the relatives walking or in carriages. Everything was in black – all the men, the women, the horses. Even when people were very poor, there were lots of carriages. The idea was to send the deceased off well. They would have had a wake to say their goodbyes. Mother used to tell the story of the woman who was dying and she asked for a favour of her husband: when her funeral took place, would he please ride in the same carriage as her mother. Obviously the husband didn't like the mother. He replied, 'There are many things I would do for you, Brigid, but, you know, if I did that it would spoil my whole day.'

We went to Punchestown, a Point-to-Point racecourse. I remember outside the gates was the most incredible collection of beggars and crippled people, all gathered there, with their hands out for money. I was horrified. We had to walk among them and through them to get to the gates. Years later, when I was going to Trinity, I was invited to go to the races at Punchestown. I accepted, but I dreaded it, because of that childhood memory. However, there was no sign of anyone begging at the gate. By that time there were, at last, some social services.

We did have one other trip to town. We went to the Provost's House in Trinity College. Provost Bernard was there. He was a second cousin of my father's, and he invited us in to lunch. I remember being very impressed with this. I was wearing what mother used to call my 'sixty horsepower dress.' It was a very warm, woolly dress with some mauve in it, and it scratched. It was high up to the neck, and I didn't like it. Provost Bernard's grandchildren, the Dobbses, were there. I remember the dining room very well. After lunch, we were sent up to the saloon, and there we played badminton! Shuttlecocks flew around in all directions.

I was very upset as we left Ireland. I was puzzled, for my mother was crying bitterly as she left my grandmother, and I didn't understand what was happening. And I didn't like being on the boat, because I got seasick. My mother had never been seasick in her life, and she couldn't understand it. The crossing took us up to ten days. When the boat reached the St Lawrence Seaway, it took us further up the St Lawrence River, which we had not seen coming away because it had been wintertime and the River had been frozen up. It was very good to get home to Bowness from the trip. While we had been away in Ireland, my father had made us a see-saw and a swing. I don't remember being homesick when I was away, but I recall being very glad to get back home.

3

OTTAWA AND FASSETT 1925–32

About the time that I was born, my father's fieldwork as Dominion Land Surveyor in Alberta had been completed. He moved into an office building in downtown Calgary, in the Thomas Block on 2nd Street at 7th Avenue, continuing to work for the Federal Government. In 1925, Dad was sent to work for the Federal Department of the Interior, in Ottawa.

Dad went on ahead, and it was a big upheaval for the family to follow. Mother had been in bed with a goitre since her youngest had been born in February, 1925. Now, it was October, and she was able to be up and about. We packed up the house, and we moved five children across the continent, three days' travel by train. Father had found a house to rent, but it wasn't available to us for five days, so we lived in the Chateau Laurier, the most prestigious hotel in Canada. I was miserable there, and I learned it was no fun for a child, living in a hotel.

Finally we could move into our house, which was on Golden Street in Highland Park, about five miles out from town. The house was not quite big enough for us. There were some nice rooms, but not enough of them. We did have a resident maid, but we were five small children. I was the eldest by four years and I was nine. There was a field out in front of the house, where my father wanted us to play cricket. No other children played cricket, so I refused, causing upset.

We used to sleep on the veranda upstairs, until November, even when it snowed. The phone had a private line with its own ringing. There was a streetcar at the bottom of the hill.

My father's new office was in the Geodetic Survey Section. This new job was a demotion, as he had been a topographical surveyor, and now he really didn't have enough to do. So he took up going to the archives, and eventually he wrote a book on the early fur trade of Canada. He was always interested in historical things, and he took me with him on investigations. He would go into graveyards with his long trousers and his good strong boots, striding ahead. I remember trying to follow. Anytime I think of looking up monuments in graveyards, I think of how the nettles stung my ankles. With sandals and maybe not even socks, I would be struggling along after my Dad. He would also go and talk to people, making notes about them. One day he said, 'Did you notice how I asked every question at least twice, so that I could be quite sure that they were telling me how it was, and not some slightly made-up situation? That's the only safe way to get information.'

We were very interested in politics, and my mother took us to the House of Commons about once a month. We got to know the politicians' personalities and all the subjects that came up in the debates. We weren't very mature with it, in that we liked somebody who made us laugh. The Prime Minister was Conservative, and he had come from New Brunswick, but he had made his name as a lawyer in Calgary. Before my parents had married, my father had shared with him the amenities of a boarding house in Calgary. So we had a personal interest in Prime Minister Richard Bedford Bennett, or Richard Bonfire Bennett as the populace called him.

I found school in Ottawa wonderful. One of the reasons I liked school so much was that I had such good friends who didn't live far away. I could see them frequently. I went first to the primary school, a public school. The bell would ring and we would line up outside the doors of the school, the girls at the girls' side, and the boys at the boys' side. The door would be opened to let us in, and we would march up to our classroom. There were 2 lines of us girls, and one line went to one classroom, and the other line went to a room opposite ours. There was one girl in the other line that I used to admire tremendously — she looked very pretty and very nice. Why wasn't I allowed into the other classroom? We didn't get to know each other then.

My parents were still not quite happy with Canadian general education, and they heard of an Irishwoman, Mrs Nancy Connell, who was setting up a private school. One of her parents had been Irish, but she had grown up in England, and gone to Cambridge University. As far as I know she had also gone to Trinity, in Dublin, and got a degree there. She used to write plays for children. I was eventually sent to this very small school. There were only about four girls my age, up to 14 years old, and one of the girls was the same girl that I had admired so much earlier in the school line-ups. It was Helen Fosbery. We became great friends, our parents became friends and they used to visit back and forth. They discovered one time when we were talking, that we were full third cousins. Her father, Harry Fosbery, was of Irish descent and they mentioned a house belonging to the Lennons down in County Meath in Ireland, and that was where we had come from, too. So that cemented my friendship with Helen. My mother was Cousin Eva to Helen, and we always called Helen's mother Cousin Margaret. And there was Cousin Harry, Helen's father. Nowadays, you'd all be on first names very quickly, but that was the way it was then. And I still correspond with Helen. I see her every time I go to Toronto, where she now lives.

I was at the private school for about a year and a half. We were called 'GELPS', Grey Lodge pupils. It was a maverick school. Mrs Connell was a very cultured woman, but I'm not sure what the programme was. The Maths was not taught well, and I don't remember what we did in Science. There were two other girls of our generation, and then mostly younger siblings of the older girls. We wore a brown tunic uniform and a beige blouse and a tie, which was half orange and half yellow. It was a crocheted tie, with a little fastener at the back. There was a very relaxed atmosphere, with gentle people and pleasant parents. Everybody was looking for a more cultured education, I suppose. Mrs Connell went for a holiday one summer to England, where she had relations, and then we were all informed that the school was closing, that it wouldn't be opening again in September. Just like that.

It was very difficult because Nepean High School, where Helen and I eventually went, was full up. Term had started before this happened, and they said they couldn't take us. My father, who never took 'no' for an answer, said that was nonsense, that we could have just moved in there from somewhere else, and what provision did they have for people who came in from another place? The High School Principal was a bit annoyed that my father made such a fuss. This man, who was D. O. Arnold and who was really quite nice, got so upset at one point in the interview that he got up and switched off the light! Eventually, an inspector came out to the school, and he put Helen and me at a table. He gave us some sums to do, and I forget what else. He was a Scotsman called Maxwell, a big burly man who blustered around the room. It really was a rather terrifying experience for us. Eventually, he said to me, 'Well, what are *you* worried about? You will be all right.' Helen wasn't as far on as I was, so she

17

was put in a lower form, where she got on very well. She had a gift for English. She used to write poems and sometimes stories. It was Maths that bothered her. I was put ahead, and that was the end of it. Both of us had got into the school and we were still together. We were there for two years.

My mother and father set off one summer's day from Hull, just across the river from Ottawa, into French country. They boarded the train, and they went on the winding rail towards Montreal. They were both good walkers, so about half way along they got off the train, and they started to walk along the road towards the next station. They called in at every farmhouse that they passed, looking for somewhere we could stay as a family, for a holiday. They found a place. A widower, whose parents lived not too far away, said he was prepared to vacate his farmhouse for two months in the summertime. This was, of course, among the French Canadians, and the whole idea of the exercise was that we should get to know French, and the French Canadian culture. After our first two summers there, the village of Fassett spoke English, having really not spoken it before at any time, and we were a little bit short on our French!

Without Dad, we were quite a party, the six of us. My father used to come down by train for weekends from Ottawa, where he was working. We often had friends with us as well. We slept on mattresses on the veranda. It was very healthy. The cows were milked very early, and then the milk was put into a churn, and a horse and trap would take it to the cheese factory. If we got up early we could go in the trap with the milk. We have always been very glad that we went to French Canada, because there has been a great deal of bitterness among people in some places, between French and English Canadians. We never became involved because we knew the French Canadians personally.

'Habitants' is the old name for them, and they were farming people. My mother and the farmer had many long talks. One time he said to her, 'The price of hay has gone up. There must be a war in Europe.' This was in 1930. They were fearful of conscription. They showed us the hideouts where they had hidden in the 1914 War, so that no-one would know there was an able-bodied man in that house. The farmer also told my mother that his sister was a nun, married to God. She wore a ring. 'And that makes God my brother-in-law,' he said.

When the French colonised Quebec, they made long, narrow farms. They liked to be close together, generally on a river, with one farm house not very far from the next one. This was very important in the winter when they were so isolated by extremely cold weather, and it gave them a sense of community.

The farm we stayed on was one of these farms, and the countryside stretched for a mile back to the Laurentian Mountains, where maple syrup was collected in the Spring. And we *loved* it. There is a lot to be said for children going to a farm. There were horses to pull in the hay. We would collect the hay as best we could from the little haystacks, and pile it up on top of the huge wagon. The horses pulled fairly slowly, and we kept sliding off and clambering back up as the horses went along. We used to stook the oats. The farm family worked hard, but it was a manageable farm. Unfortunately there was a lot of TB among those people. The farmer's first wife had died from it, and his eldest daughter was in decline. She just languished with her grandparents, and everyone knew that she was going to die, as had her mother four or five years before.

The Church was very strong; perhaps an echo of what was going on in Ireland at that time. One year there was a plague in Ottawa of what we called 'Infantile Paralysis', now known as polio. My father was dreadfully worried, so we stayed on in Fassett an extra month, September, and then on into October, although school had started September 1st. The priest came to see the farmer, to tell him under no circumstances were any of us to go near their school.

When I went back after about thirty years there was a lot of talk about how everybody should be able to speak both English and French. It has made some difference. At that time, an Albertan farmer from the 'Bible Belt' in Canada was heard on national radio to declare 'if English was good enough for Jesus Christ, it is good enough for me.'

Years later, when Don and I were holidaying in Canada, we drove down to Fassett to see where we had been for summer holidays. In a big shop in the main street we asked for directions to our farmer friends. I had been sixteen when I had last seen their family, and by this time I was well into my fifties. We drove out to their house, parked the car and walked up and rang the bell. The wife came to the door . She stared for a moment, and then she threw her arms around me and said, 'Daphné!' I was very touched. She immediately got on the phone to her daughter whom I had known as a little girl, who now lives in Montreal, and said some words in French, 'Daphné this' and 'Daphné that.' We hadn't been in the house five minutes, and she said she would like to give us a nice French lunch. Meanwhile, she sent us off in the car to the actual house where we had stayed before for the summers. We went down to explore the river where we used to swim so much, a wide river with a good beach. There were always very happy memories at Fassett.

When Bennett became Prime Minister, it was essential that he cut down

19

on expenses. This was in the depth of the depression which had started in the States in 1929, and by the thirties it had reached Canada. My father was declared redundant, and was given compulsory retirement. I was the eldest at 16, and there were four below me at very expensive ages. Dad had no compunction about going to see his former boarding house mate Prime Minister R. B. Bennett for help. Bennett arranged for my father to have a job in the Department of Natural Resources, but only for a year, to help recover from the shock. Dad had a very wide knowledge of the outdoors, because he had surveyed in the wild for so long, and he had good general knowledge overall. He spent a lot of his time writing little snippets to put into the newspaper, mostly on Canadian geography or wild animals. We used to scan the paper to find something that he had put in. But one year later, in 1932, all that was concluded. Dad had to retire. We had to take the train and go back to Calgary, much to my grief. The condition of the Bowness house after seven years wasn't too bad, and it provided a roof for us. My father's pension wasn't very good, and we were very hard up at that time.

It was very sad that I had to leave Ottawa, because it really was my place to be at that time. D. O. Arnold, the Principal, a very small man, had been very good to us. He and his wife used to take Helen and me out for picnics. There was a matriculation exam at 16/17 years, but I had to leave before taking it. One of the subjects that we would have done in the later years was Ancient History, and I had been looking forward to that. But when we moved to Calgary, Ancient History was taken in the first year of High School, so I missed out on the subject yet again. For many reasons, having to leave my life in Ottawa was traumatic for me.

4

EXTRACTS FROM 'JOTTY,' DAPHNE'S FIRST DIARY 1930–32

(**Daphne, 13 years old in March, 1930 calls herself 'Waffy.' 'Pluffy' means 'Pouff! I'm gone!'**)

During the winter Helen and I had buried an ink-bottle in the snow, near the school fence. Shortly afterwards Helen started a diary. She wanted me to do so as well, so I said I would when the snow melted and the bottle was unburied. Today, Helen found the bottle uncovered, and she told me I had to start my own diary (called 'Jotty'). So I am!

Sunday, March 30th, 1930 (in Ottawa)

We had the Litany in church this morning. Just before it began, Mother leaned over to me and whispered, 'Who is the third girl in the front row of the choir?' I told her I did not know, and she said nothing. I am afraid, Jotty, I did not pay much attention to the remainder of the service, for my mind was too busily engaged, thinking about this mysterious girl. Of course, I looked eagerly at the third girl, but, strange to say, she did not look very romantic. The big questions were 'Who is she? A long lost relative? An heiress? A criminal sought for by the police? Was she lame? Deaf? Blind?'

These and many others were the questions that I asked myself. As soon as I was out of the church, I ran up to Mother who was ahead of me, and said, as calmly as I could, 'Why did you ask me who the third girl in the choir was?' 'Oh', she replied, 'I think she is rather 'cute-looking', and I wanted you to notice her, and perhaps be able to tell me who she is!'

Was I disgusted? Why wasn't she a long-lost relative? An heiress? An innocent criminal? Or something more thrilling than just 'cute-looking'?

It's ten now, and I must go to sleep. *Pluffy*

Wednesday, April 2ⁿᵈ, 1930 (in Ottawa)

Today, Mother, Dorothy and I walked to Aunt Jane's, Dad's sister's place, and had tea. We walked all the way – remember, Jotty, it is about four miles. We got to Aunt's room at three, had tea, and arrived home at half-past five. The main feature of the afternoon was Aunt putting the tea-pot on the table ready for tea, when she had not put any water in it.

Coming up the street we met Daddy, and I almost wish we hadn't. When we came to the corner, there was a car, and we were not sure whether it was going to go straight on, or turn. Anyway, we ran across, but Daddy stood stock-still in the middle of the road. Naturally the car had to stop, and I'm not sure what Daddy shouted. Something about 'the idea of running down children.' Ahem! And me nearly fourteen! As if *I* were a child! Ha!

Tonight, however, was 'the best.' We went to the Parish Hall to hear H. H. Stevens speak on 'Britain, the Cradle of Christianity.' At the end, Mr Steacy said, 'This speech has left me gasping. I haven't gasped so much since the night Mrs Steacy said "Yes".' After, he said, 'I know there are many Anglicans here, but there are also people of other denominations, and to make them feel at home, we shall pass around the plate.'

Val doesn't like me having the light on, so I'll have to turn it off, and say, dear Jotty, *Pluffy*

Friday, August 15ᵗʰ, 1930 (on holiday, in Fassett, Quebec)

It must be at least five weeks since I told you anything at all. Poor Jotty! So much has been going on in the world and you, tucked away in a drawer, have not the slightest idea of what we have been doing all this time.

My reason for having neglected you for so long is we're away on holidays and Helen is here. She is so perfect! It is impossible to tell you any decent news in a short time. Helen would have been left at a loose end while I was with you, so I thought it would be better to wait till some time when I was alone. That time has come now.

One of Mother's friends wrote and said she *might* be down this afternoon by the bus. It is due to arrive in twenty minutes, and I am going to meet it. I really must go up now to meet the bus. Love till later, Waffy, *Pluffy*

Friday, August 22nd, 1930 (in Fassett)

It's a whole week since I gave you any news, so I'll have more than ever to tell you. Although the lady did not come by the bus, I didn't return to you, and here is my reason. While I was waiting for the bus, and *wishing the hurry would bust*, my cow, the one I usually milk, came up to the gate and stood there. There is no water in the cow's field, so I thought I couldn't bear to come home, and leave the poor thing without anything to drink. I knew that you'd rather I bring water to the cow, than tell you the news, so I carried up one pail. It was hard work, too, up the steep hill to the bus stop. The cow, Emily, drank the water after a short time, and she seemed very thirsty. I then brought her another pail, which she also took. After that I carried up another, which I had taken from a barrel outside. Emily had wandered some distance away from the gate, so thinking she would like more to drink, I placed the pail of water on a ledge and I sat down to wait for the bus. I was looking down the road one minute – the next, at my drenched self. I was soaked. Of course, you know what happened. The pail on the rickety ledge had tipped over on to me. I got up rather disgustedly, and walked home with the empty pail. I looked round. Emily had reached the gate, and looked disappointed. Really, I don't know which I was sorrier for – poor Emily who did not get her drink, or for myself. Bye for now, Jotty, *Pluffy*

Saturday, August 30th, 1930 (in Fassett)

For once, Jotty, you may rejoice, as I have done what I said I would. I have an hour and five minutes for you, and I hope to make good use of it. This morning, out on the veranda in bed, I was writing a letter. The ink bottle was beside my mattress, and Brian, coming out of the front door, tripped and spilled the ink all over the place. I felt a cold spot on my back. I tried to make myself believe it was Brian's fault at first, but naturally, it was my own. Mother had warned me not to spill the ink, and I had said I was sure I wouldn't. Little I knew! Of course, *I* did not spill it, but I'm afraid I'll never allow myself to write another letter in bed, unless I am not feeling well. It is a pity, too, because I love writing letters there, early in the morning. The damage, however, was awful. Ink spattered all over both ends of the flannelette blanket, and my embroidered pillowcase, which matches my bedroom set, had its share. Brian's pillowcase was sprayed blue. There was a large spot on the back of my pyjamas. The ink has also disfigured the paint on the veranda and on the outside wall of the house. Mother says the things can be 'unstained' by salts of lemon, but I wish it had never happened. Oh! Yes! I know it is my fault now. How could Brian help what he did?

I have ten minutes to waken the children, dress them, dress myself, and get up to the bus. Now, in haste, *Pluffy*

Sunday, August 31st, 1930 (in Fassett)

This evening I milked my own dear Emily. The children are in bed. I lost my temper with Val, and gave her a whacking. She would not hurry, and I was annoyed. She says I hurt her thumb, by bending it back. It is half past eight, and by the time I am ready for bed, it will be much later. I want to get up early to milk. At any rate I shall have to be up, for Daddy is going by the first bus and needs a breakfast.

I really must stop now. I'll drop you some news before we go home, if possible, but, Jot, for tonight, *Pluffy*

Monday, September, 1st, 1930 (in Fassett)

We are off home to Ottawa tomorrow morning! I have had a feeling all the time we would go. Now, Jotty, from your sleepy Waffy, *Pluffy*

Thursday, January 8th, 1931 (in Ottawa)

I felt so decidedly *punk* last night that I just tumbled into bed, dear Jotty, without even washing! About twenty past nine last night, suddenly my head began to ache, my neck felt as if it had four or five swollen glands in it, my throat began to feel sore, my back ached, and my eyes got weak, so I came to the hasty conclusion that bed was the best place for me. I told Helen about it today, and she laughed and said, 'Did someone imagine this for you, or did you do all the imagining yourself?'

This part is written tomorrow morning. Just as I was writing 'imagining', I heard Daddy coming up. I had to hurriedly finish, cover the ink, and turn off my light. Dad would be fierce if he found me with my light on at that hour. It is 7.10 a.m. now. I am giving Val her spelling, and I shall soon have to get up.

Saturday should be a busy day for me. Here's what I should do, but I'll be lucky if I get it half done. Do some housework, peel vegetables, wash, have my piano lesson, and practise afterwards, go to town, write two letters, write a composition, do *some* of my homework, give the children a bath, and catch up some accounts! Enough, isn't it? Oh, sure! From Waffy, *Pluffy*

Tuesday, January 20th, 1931 (in Ottawa)

Mother fell all the way down the back stairs today, and hurt her leg and shoulder very badly. While she was falling, she said she was thinking, 'I'm dead, I'm quite dead.' It really is a wonder she isn't! When she got to the bottom, in answer to Brian's enquiry, 'Oh, Mother, what happened?' she said, 'Oh, I'm all right. I feel good, I feel good.' *Pluffy*

Thursday, February 19th, 1931 (in Ottawa)

I have determined to turn off my light in seven minutes, so here goes. Mother and I went to a tea party, and had a good time. There was another girl there, who was passing round tea as well. At first I felt dreadfully shy, but by the time we parted we were quite good friends. There were hundreds of people there, over twenty anyway, and so we were kept busy. *Pluffy*

Wednesday, February 25th, 1931 (in Ottawa)

Mother was not feeling well today, so she stayed in bed. The children were rather boisterous.

Last night, it was late when I came upstairs. I found I had forgotten the ink, but I did not want to risk going down into the dining room where Dad was, to get it. He was mad this evening, over the top, because it was 9:45 when I came up. He said I would be wearing glasses in no time. He brought up the old subject of how he always went to bed early when he was my age, and got up at 6 a.m. He and Aunt Jane are very fond of harping on that subject. Bologna! *Pluffy*

Sunday, March 8th, 1931 (in Ottawa)

I think I shall start by telling you about what happened to Aunt Jane last night. You see it was a terrible night out, a snow storm was raging and Aunt Jane came here in a taxi. When the driver got to the corner he thought that he never could get up this road, so Aunt got out, and began to walk home. She managed quite well until she tumbled into a snowdrift. She sank up to her waist in snow. She told us she finally picked herself out, and then went to ask for help! In the end, a neighbour had to bring her over, both wearing snowshoes. Imagine it! It is only a few feet from here to there. Big drifts are all over the creation. *Pluffy*

Saturday, January 2nd, 1932 (in Ottawa)

You've been left in a cupboard a long time, Jotty! I got an invitation from my friend Bertha today to a birthday dance in a week. Now, you know, Jotty, Dad never lets me out at night, let alone to a dance! Heavenly Day! He'd have a fit. I began to cry when I read the 'invite,' I just couldn't help it. It makes me *so* angry, this idea of caging us all up. One of these days I'm going to quit. I'll either have to write to Bert, and explain matters just as they are, or else 'sneak out.' Of course, I'd far rather do the latter, but it would mean such a lot of anxiety for Mother for fear Dad would find out. Anyway, it would take days to persuade her that Dad wouldn't discover it. Then, too, I haven't much idea of dancing.

I'd so love to go. It's a rotten life. I haven't shown the letter to Mother yet; I didn't want to worry her. *Pluffy*

Friday, January 22nd, 1932 (in Ottawa)

Dad was on the warpath again tonight. Nothing serious, but he was just cross. He was tired, and he complained of suffocating and of not feeling well. But when he starts being cross, it makes me think of the bad stuff. I'm terrified of being dumb and a wallflower. There's nothing I'd hate worse. I know the boys think I'm *daft*. Helen got to go out tonight, and she gets to go out again next Friday. I'm not grudging her a bit, but I do wish I could get out. Do I ever! I send my very best love, Jot *Pluffy*

Friday, January 29th, 1932 (in Ottawa)

Everyone's out tonight and here I am stuck inside, with Dad in a moody temper because I didn't start to go to bed until ten. I was writing. He came into the breakfast room, looked at the clock, and said, 'You'll pay for this in a couple of years'. I grinned inwardly. There is a ski hike at the school tonight – I've longed to go to it. Then there is a party tonight, and a whole lot of kids are going. And here am I.

I'm a sap, eh, Jot? *Pluffy*

Monday, February 8th, 1932 (in Ottawa)

Mother went out today, and I had to get supper. Everything went very well until we started supper. You know, Jotty, the children are *supposed* to obey me. I try to be firm about this, and usually succeed. My one fear about being a teacher is that I won't be able to keep order. So I must practise being a disciplinarian now. See? I didn't know how to behave towards the children. I gave Val and Brian sort of lectures, but they didn't listen to a word.

Later, I had to get Mother's supper, and I haven't had a moment since. I wonder if the children will be better or worse next time? Eh? *Pluffy*

Monday, February 15th, 1932 (in Ottawa)

You know, Jot, I'm just going wild for excitement or variation of some kind. I feel like a cooped chicken. I do wish Dad was the sort of person who wouldn't mind hundreds coming in here for parties. Another bad thing is not being allowed out at night. I know I've harped on this subject a hundred times, but I'm nearly crazy. I have to ask Dad 'to allow' me to go to the school concert. I wanted to do it, and get it over with tonight, but didn't get a chance. Just imagine how glorious it would be to be able to stay out as late as I liked without encountering a bear when I got home. Too good to be true.

Mum went to town. Children good. Love, Waffy. *Pluffy*

Sunday, February 21st, 1932 (in Ottawa)

In Sunday School, just when I got in, Bert told me she went to a tea yesterday, and ate two dozen pieces of short bread. When we were saying a prayer within which were the words 'Pardon our shortcomings', Bert said, 'Oh, pardon my shortbread!' I nearly died, but when, in the Lord's Prayer, she said 'Give us this day our daily shortbread' and 'Deliver us from shortbread,' I did. It was a terrible example for the kids, and they were shocked. *Pluffy*

Monday, February 22nd, 1932 (in Ottawa)

As Mother wasn't feeling well, she went to bed. There's been a good deal for me to do consequently. This evening, Dad was as cross as two bears. No doubt he was feeling out of sorts, but nevertheless, he damned the scissors and iodine because he couldn't find them, cursed my folly when I poured cold instead of hot water into his orange juice, and damnationed and

27

vigorously slammed the cabinet door when he bumped his head against it. *Pluffy*

Saturday, February 27th, 1932 (in Ottawa)

There's a school dance going on now. Of course, I couldn't stay for that. I must tell you about the fuss about my going to town today. I couldn't possibly have let Dad know where I was going, and it was ages before Mother would consent to my doing it on the sly. She finally did. It meant I had to get off the streetcar early, take the bus, and then transfer to another streetcar. It also meant *heart failure* for me the whole time I was in town for fear I should encounter Dad. If only I had known he was at home, I wouldn't have nearly fainted when we transferred. However, *Ende gut, alles gut*. It was about *twelve* last night, when I *se couched*. Love, Waffy *Pluffy*

Saturday, March 5th, 1932 (in Ottawa)

Mary's in my class, and I went into her place on the streetcar today to study Physics. When I was coming home up the street I met Mum going to the village, so I joined her. We had to search the place for 3½" nails, but we came home without them. We weren't back until after dark. Dad hadn't known where I was, and had raised Cain about me going out alone and being kidnapped. Nut! Poor Hugh had to 'phone the post office *'n everythin'*. Dad went for Mum when we got back. Poor Mum is always the goat. She gave as good back, though. Waffy's tired, *Pluffy*

Monday, March 7th, 1932 (in Ottawa, soon after learning they would be leaving)

I'm already beginning to feel homesick. Mother mentioned Helen and my eyes filled with tears! Nuts, eh? Mary can't get over it at all, and said she hasn't been able to sleep properly since. Every one is learning about it. I still don't know whether or not Helen knows. Gosh! I'll begin to cry if this keeps on! From a sad Waffy, *Pluffy*

Tuesday, March 8th, 1932 (in Ottawa)

I signed myself as a sad Waffy last night, but then I had nothing to complain about. Jotty, I've lost my beloved, valued fountain pen. I'm sick with worry and misery. I love it almost as much as I do Cotter, our cat, and whatever will I do in the exams? Oh! Jot! I'm almost bawling! When I got home and took off my tunic, I could only find the top of my pen. I went to look along

the path, but no trace. The snow has drifted, too. Oh! Jot! I'm nearly crazy.
Pluffy

Sunday, March 13th, 1932 (in Ottawa)

I went to bed early last night, but nevertheless when I turned off the light
for Dad, I fell asleep. I truly am as sorry as can be, and I'll try to make up
now. It's about 7:15 a.m., I'm sitting up in bed, and I have to get up in a few
minutes to iron a blouse for myself.

Yesterday morning I did a big washing, and afterwards traced some
baskets and loaves and fishes for the Sunday School kids. The minister gets
older every day, face going in, eyes coming out. Queer churchwarden, fat at
back all sticking out.

I wrote part of a letter tonight. Mother went out to visit, and I got supper.
Everything was perfect until near the end, when Dad began to wash up. He
broke a tumbler and a saucer, and had the dishes all over the shelf when
Mum came in. I began to cry, because I was so anxious for there to be no
fuss when she arrived. I haven't heard from Helen today. All are well, Jot.
Are you? Sweet dreams, *Pluffy*

Friday, April Fool's Day, 1932 (in Ottawa)

It's a queer world, and the queerest and hardest thing to put up with about
it, is – Dad! Dad was told by Muv that I was out. Then Mum went into the
village. When she got home, Dad came out yelling, wanting to know where
I was, and that I mustn't be out after six. When I got in, I was feeling
particularly happy and carefree, but Mother was crying inside the door. I
guessed, but yet could hardly believe why. It was broad daylight, too, for a
long time afterwards. Hugh got in at 2 minutes to six. Dad seems to pride
himself on this 'being in on the dot at six' stuff. He's a big bully – *The* big
bully. The very worst part of it is that he always goes for Mother, and
Mother's nerves are absolutely undone. When I got in, she was saying, 'Oh,
I can't stand it! I can't stand it.' She's crying now downstairs, and Dad is
sulking.

What *is* a body to do? Be in by six! *Pluffy*

Saturday, April 2nd, 1932 (in Ottawa)

The row is on the mend, but Mother looks fierce. She has looked wretched just lately, and I don't mean maybe! Dad began yelling, which set Muv off again, and she went to bed till just before dinner at two. Dad has been miserable all day, till he asked me if I were going out this aft. He said not to stay late, after what happened yesterday. I said I had been home in broad daylight. He made a face, and said the whole trouble was they didn't know whether I had got in from the walk. Crazy nonsense. He then said I should be in by *seven* in future. Rather a come down. Mum laughed. He's better since. He even crated books he declared yesterday that he would never pack. I think he dislikes rows *more* than we do. *Pluffy*

Saturday, April 9th, 1932 (in Ottawa)

I have ten minutes to write you, Jot, undress, and do my hair, so please excuse hasty writing.

Dad and I went to the Archives today at about 11:30 and we got home after 6. It wasn't too bad. I always had an idea the Archives were as old and faded as the manuscripts in it, but they're bright and interesting. We had something to eat about 2:30 at the 'Honey Dew', through whose windows I saw one of my teachers hoofing it along, as if she meant business. *Pluffy*

Sunday, April 10th, 1932 (in Ottawa)

We went to the Cathedral tonight. I have always liked the Dean. He made a couple of good jokes in his sermon, said other funny things, and freely used slang words to express himself. He said he once tried to make a joke with one of those morose bank tellers, and he was told, 'I'll refer it to the manager.' He said he would rather deliver milk at five o'clock in the morning than be a Member of Parliament. He said, 'O God, make bad people good, and good people nicer.' *Pluffy*

Thursday, April 14th, 1932 (in Ottawa)

Along comes the teacher today, sits down in front of me and asks me when are we leaving. She said she was sorry I was going, that the kids and staff would miss me. I should have said 'It's very nice of you to say so, but you're not going to miss me half as much as I'll miss you', but as usual I had no *savoir faire*. I just grinned. I also wanted to say I had been looking forward so much to having her next year, too, but perhaps I will yet, when I give her my autograph book to write in. *Sais pas. Pluffy*

Sunday, April 17th, 1932 (in Ottawa)

I'll begin about church. I 'phoned Bert and asked her to go to church. She wanted to, so we did. Dor and Val came along, too. Bert and I were not very good. We had to smile at the Rev's sermon, and to poke each other in 'love divine' hymns, but I don't think any one noticed it, even if we did shake with suppressed laughter once or twice.

Dor and Val, though, when they saw Mrs Benbow's hat! They both began to giggle like two idiots, and kept on, making such a racket. I pinched Val to try to make her cry, but she giggled worse than ever. Then things became desperate. I grabbed Val and put her between Bert and me, and at the same time a lady in the seat behind gave Dorothy a poke in the back with her umbrella. We're disgraced forever in the eyes of that church. It's just as well we have only one more Sunday there.

Dad lenient, when we were not getting home on time. Nut. *Pluffy*

Sunday, April 24th, 1932 (in Ottawa)

Today in Sunday School, the Head came in to my Primary Class, and began talking about the West. He said he used to live out there, and would like to go again. I looked over at Bert, and whispered, 'He can go in my place!' Then I grinned, chiefly at the coincidence of his mentioning the West. What was my great surprise to find out that he was leading up to my departure, and to presenting me with a book, *The Second Mile*. I was so embarrassed, but it was *terrible* nice of them. Eh, what? *Pluffy*

Monday, May 23rd, 1932 (back in Bowness, Calgary)

Almost a month since I last wrote, but oh! Jot! I find it so hard to get time for you with all the homework, the long hours I am away at school, making the lunches, and last but not least, all the holes in my stockings to be darned.

Well, we'll have the company of a cow tomorrow night. A black and white bony Holstein, called 'Liz.' We are re-christening her 'Betsy', which I think sounds a lot more elegant. So, now, added to the rest, I'll have the milking to do.

The teachers pile on the homework fast and heavy. I'm praying I'll get the exams.

Saturday, May 28th, 1932 (in Bowness)

I spent some of this morning and most of this aft. writing letters. I've been busy all this week, as I now have an extra job – the milking. Dear Betsy – she is so quiet and affectionate I don't mind at all, but everything takes time. By the way, it's exactly a month since we left Ottawa on that memorable night. Oh Jot! How I miss them all, all my dear friends, and if it weren't for their letters I believe I'd hike it back. Oh, Jot, help me not miss them so much. I'm so young and innocent. *Pluffy*

5

RETURN TO CALGARY 1932–35

I never settled in Calgary in the same way after Ottawa. I had left all my good friends behind at the age of sixteen. I didn't find equally congenial people in Calgary. But the rest of my family, who were a good deal younger than I was, loved the freedom of the people and the space of the Prairie. It was unfortunate that I didn't.

My trouble was that I had left a lovely group of people in Ottawa. I was so homesick for them. There was one girl in Calgary who went to another school. She lived not too far from where we were, and I liked her very much. She was my full twin, born on the same day, in the same year, and in Calgary, too. Her grandmother was Indian. Her father had darker colouring, but Gwenneth not so much, and she was tall and slim and graceful. Unfortunately, she wasn't in the group that went to my school, Crescent Heights High School.

We returned to the original house in Bowness, which had not been sold. We had bikes in Calgary, and if the wind wasn't strong, or if it was at your back, we felt great freedom in the fresh air from the mountains. There was no skiing in Calgary then. The region was still underdeveloped and poor.

My father had retired with a poor pension. We didn't have a lot of money for extras, and the housekeeping had to be done very carefully. Sausages were a treat, only bought if in a sale. We kept a cow, as Mum had grown up in the country, and she knew about these things. She made butter, but the churn had to be turned for a long time. My sister would tie her foot on to the handle and read a book while she churned.

I had learned on the French Canadian farm how to milk a cow, and I never regretted anything so much. Nobody else could milk, and it used to tie me down as I had to come back for milking time in the early evening. I had to put on my oldest clothes as a cow is pretty smelly when you are in close contact, milking her. The milk was kept in big pans, and we skimmed off the cream, using spoons. Sometimes people bought milk from us. We were all getting to the point of needing an education, so financially it was pretty rough.

I now attended a high school of about one thousand students. It took an hour in the streetcar to get to Crescent Heights. Other students lived nearer the town than I did, so I was the first to get on the street car, and the others got on as we went along. There was only one with whom I had any satisfactory friendship. I kept in touch with her till she died, about ten years ago. She was the one that was criticised by the others, if they got half a chance. It was unpleasant being cooped up with this group, but there was no way to separate myself from them. I just had to put up with it. They were unkind and petty, and enjoyed backbiting. I didn't know how to cope with them. I was very unhappy and very homesick for Ottawa.

We had two hours for lunch, but I couldn't possibly go home, as it took an hour each way. I used to sit with people around a table, but they weren't the kind of people I had been friendly with before. I didn't settle down and I felt very lost.

The school principal was a man called Aberhart, who eventually became Premier of Alberta. He was an Ian Paisley type. He had a church, and he used to broadcast every Sunday when he'd lay down the law. He was known to be dictatorial in school, but he placed me into an appropriate class.

One of the subjects I had to take was physics, compulsory at the time. I entered the physics classroom, and there was a rather bad-tempered man. He paid little attention to me for a day or two. Then he looked at the textbook I had used in Ottawa, found it was similar to the one he used, and realised that I would fit in. He asked me, 'Where were you at, in Ontario?' Misunderstanding the question, I replied, 'At electricity.' That made the class roar with laughter, as what he was trying to find out was where we had lived. I didn't exactly warm to him. I rang up my mother and asked her if I could drop Physics. She said that I would know best. So I went straight into

Aberhart's office, told him I wanted to drop Physics, and he gave me Biology instead.

It was the English teacher who was very gifted. Making us interested and getting us to work very hard, he brought out the best in us. He talked to each of us individually about our work, and I have always been very grateful to him.

The way they built the timetable was unusual. On the first day of school you would make your own timetable from a huge board in one room. The bell would ring and you would start to run to the room of the teacher for the first class on your own timetable. Everyone else would be running according to their timetable. If you had a special teacher that you wanted to be sure that you didn't miss, you would run very fast, in case he would be booked out by the time you got there. You went in and signed up, and that was the class list for the teacher. After a short time the bell would ring again and you would run to the next classroom. It went on and on, and it was quite entertaining. I have never known anything like it in my life, and yet it worked. Some teachers didn't get very many students at all, and, occasionally, you would miss out on a teacher that you really wanted. One term, I ended up doing English with an unpleasant, snippety teacher. But they soon got rid of her, and we got Mortimer Watts instead.

Morty Watts said, 'There is one group of people in this country who are expected to work eighteen hours a day, and that is the High School student.' That was quite true if you did the assigned homework in a conscientious way. I look on it as being a time when I was very pushed. In the summer, because of moving from one end of the country to another, I had to prepare for supplementals in French, which I couldn't fit into my school timetable.

I did have a further year's education at the school, after I graduated. That was counted as first year University. We studied Calculus, and other higher level courses. Second year University was offered in Calgary by Mount Royal College, a Methodist Foundation. The University of Alberta recognised two years' credit for this combination. The University of Alberta was up in Edmonton. A number of people who had been at school in Calgary, and whose parents could not afford the fees plus the room and board costs required to attend the University, were sent instead to Mount Royal College in Calgary. Later, when I started in Dublin University, I had what was called in Alberta, two years University, and they were recognised in Dublin as one year University. So I came in to Trinity as a Senior Freshman.

There were some very good students at Mount Royal College, some of them quite mature as they had already been out teaching in schools. We were instructed by a very good History teacher, and I'm sure it was because of him that later I was content to take History in Trinity. We also studied Economics and English.

I used to have to leave home at 7 a.m., to walk a mile across the prairie to where my friend, whose grandfather had been an Indian, was living. Her father had to be at work very early, and they had a car, so I got a lift into town. It was a long day, especially in the winter.

Most of the students then went on to finish at the University of Alberta, in Edmonton. My family could not afford to send me. It was clear that my two brothers would get the education, for they had to support a family in the future. We didn't question those things then. I didn't know what was going to be my future, what I was going to do.

Then I received a cable from my Aunt Olive, my mother's sister in Ireland, asking me to go over to Ireland and stay with her for the summer. Olive had married the local doctor, Charles Ross of Navan, a much respected GP. They were first cousins, their mothers being sisters. They had known each other all their lives, and Charles had been in his fifties and Olive in her thirties when they married. Charles hadn't been well. He had been in hospital when he had had an x-ray burn to his back in the early 1930s, a time when they were still experimenting with the procedure. The burn had turned to cancer, and he had died from it nine months after they were married.

It had left my aunt in an awful state. She hadn't been fully informed as to the severity of Charles' condition. His death had come as a dreadful shock to her, and she was now living on her own in the country. So I happily went over to stay with her for six months.

6

BROWNSTOWN HOUSE, COUNTY MEATH 1935

Daphne is 19 years old

> *Thursday, May 23rd (on the train from Calgary to Montreal)*
Thought I had missed Lake Superior, and the view Dad had shown us when we were going to Ottawa, in 1925. I was thrilled when it appeared suddenly from behind a forest of firs and leafless poplars. The purple hills in the distance were dim and yet clearly outlined. The sun was shining on the water very brightly, and the trees growing on the picturesque islands seemed ready to fall off into the water. Lake Superior lasted until late morning. All day, little lakes and rivers suddenly appeared from behind the trees. Some of the rivers were sandy and some clear, and wild ducks bobbed like little boats in the water.

> *Sunday, May 26th (on the boat from Montreal to Belfast)*
I have a new friend, Florence. We skipped church and went to the gym instead – what fun! If we had that paraphernalia in our basement at home I might be thin. First we rode a mile on a bicycle, then we trotted on a horse, and after that we rowed across the lake. Next, we had our livers massaged for about ten minutes, after which we threw a basketball filled with lead, hither

and yon. Finally, we had a rub down, and ran to our cabins with bare legs, just as the good people of the boat were filing out of church. I had to be very careful not to let my two cabin companions know where I had been – I don't think they ever suspected the awful truth. They came in to change their shoes when I still had my shorts on under my kimono. 'I suppose you're dressing for church?' enquired one. I didn't tell a lie, but I quickly changed the subject.

This afternoon we saw two icebergs to the south and Labrador to the north. No Newfoundland! The icebergs were beauties – all they lacked was a polar bear standing on top. One was in two parts – it looked like the top of a castle. The other was large and had a tail that stretched back many miles. The lens of my camera was so dirty with salt spray I couldn't get a picture of them.

Saturday, June 1st

I was just finishing dressing yesterday when I saw a funnel appear at the porthole window. The tender was there! I never ran up some stairs so quickly as I did to the deck. There was a crowd jammed up against the railing to see the tender and also to watch a Dodge vehicle being lowered from the steamer. I made good use of my elbows through the crowd and I got to the edge. I'm sure some good people will be black and blue today. I looked desperately at all the passengers on the tender, and at first all I could see was one person whom I thought might be Grannie. Then I suddenly saw Aunt Olive, so recently widowed and, behind her, Uncle Charlie, her brother. I screamed frantically, but it was quite three minutes before they saw me. They had been looking but had given up in despair, thinking that either I was seasick or I was not on board.

The customs was quite an ordeal. I was worried stiff because I had boxes of chocolates. I was taken into a large stone room, like a stable – not that it was dirty, but it was exceedingly large and bare. There were trellises where they put our trunks, each under its own initial on the wall. I had to unrope mine, while my temperature rose by hundreds of degrees. The chocolates were found, but were passed.

The trunk was tied to the back of Uncle's Austin, using Betsy's rope, the one she had been tethered with back in Calgary. Immediately, through the city streets, we set out for Brownstown House, in Kentstown, near Navan. Belfast is well spread out along the river. It is so pretty to see the houses with the emerald hills behind them.

We drove round the City Hall – Uncle Charlie said Dad would remember when it was built. Belfast has had great doings during the past few weeks for the Jubilee celebrations, and was very crowded. Aunt and Uncle had booked rooms for yesterday at a hotel sometime before, but by the time they claimed them, the rooms had been given to someone else. They had to sleep in the stock rooms. There the beds were tables with a couple of sheets thrown across them, and there wasn't even a mirror in the ladies' dressing room.

It was a marvellous drive down to Brownstown House. The fields were picturesque and green, although there was talk of drought the past month. The hedges were beautiful, the hawthorn was in bloom. Every once in a while we saw a rhododendron. Then as we got further south we saw yellow gorse. We passed through all kinds of places that I couldn't begin to get my tongue around (that's Irish or nothing), let alone remember the names. We stopped off at Newry for some tea at the Imperial Hotel. It was delicious and so quickly made. We seemed to walk in and then have toast follow us. The waitress was very Irish-looking and spoke with a strong accent. She stood attentively by the door all the time. That bothered me, but maybe it shouldn't have.

There is such a short distance between each place, and it is built up all the way along the road. There are some thatched roofs left, but they are quickly disappearing. Whitewash is still the favourite paint. There are new little labourers' cottages, quite gay, but as Uncle says, not too fancy. Many people from the south-west coast are being put on the land.

Girls ride bicycles. They dress like Canadians, perhaps not quite so particular, but the thing I noticed was their clear, rosy complexions.

As Aunt Olive says, Brownstown House is in the heart of the country, being close to Navan. It doesn't seem that way to me, because it is so shut in by the trees and hedges. I was more than anxious to see the house, for I expected great things and I'm not disappointed. From the outside the house is not particularly attractive. It is square cut, with cream stucco, very large windows, and not much of a veranda. But inside! The drawing room is a dream. It is all done in green. Are the ceilings ever a mile up! Large green curtains on the huge windows and green coverings for the chairs. The view is magnificent, and the furniture is perfect, too. I was just looking at a closing card table that is beautiful, even in its closed state. The staircase is the width of my outstretched arms, and the halls below are huge. Aunt Olive's room is in gold, trimmed with autumn-coloured curtains. Her table-set is green with all sorts of mirrors. The pictures are splendid. The breakfast room, opposite the drawing room, is where we have our meals. The dining room is a huge place, with a large table and a magnificent chandelier with candles. We use lamps in our bedroom. There is a lovely table lamp in the drawing room. It is surprising how little you find yourself inconvenienced by lamps, even after all the electric lights we use at home. All kinds of old silver, and beautiful curios. If I had the time, energy, and ambition I could go on for longer.

The marvellous garden is enclosed by an old wall, along the top of which grows a sample of every kind of flower. Plum and cherry trees climb the wall on the inside – they will soon have to be netted. There are ample trees just past the blooming state all over the garden. Flowers grow along the central path and all over the first quarter as you go in. The rest is vegetables except for the greenhouse and the odd rockery. There are boxwood borders, where the tulips are just past their best, and where the irises are coming on.

The tulips are gigantic – I never saw anything like them. They come up to my waist and their blooms are as large as big cups. Also gooseberry bushes (we had gooseberry fool the first night), red, white and black currant bushes, raspberry canes, and masses of strawberries which will very soon be ripe. Then it will be a case of 'bend down sister if you want to get thin'.

Outside the entrance to the garden is a most attractive avenue of trees, at the end of which is a perfect view of the ruins of Skryne Castle on a hill. From the other side of the house you can just see the top of the monastic ruins on the Hill of Slane. The weathercock on the stable says 1720.

The house itself is built on the foundations of an old castle. It is romantic downstairs, but dark and musty. Down there is the wine cellar with large compartments for six different kinds of wine, and a little china sign by each cubby hole giving the name of the wine. Another separate cool place is for hanging meat. Then there is a room where three beds are jammed in a row against the wall – evidently the maids' room. In the cellar hall stands a real, old mangle – the kind you fill full of stones, but this one is filled full of bottles. I never thought you really mangled with stones before. The bells in the kitchen are fascinating. There are eight of them, one for each main room. When a bell cord is pulled, the bell rings, and its spring keeps moving after the ringing has ceased so that the maids can tell in which room they are wanted. The front doorbell is now out of order – we need my brother Brian's expertise.

A gorgeous copper beech gracefully grows outside one drawing room window, and a monkey-puzzle tree outside another. Of course, there are all kinds of horse chestnuts, oaks, elms, with an occasional fir tree too.

The birds are lovely. Very early in the morning, they frequently wake me up and each time I listen to them for about half an hour. Saw a stonechat this morning, carrying a worm to its nest in the wall. The pigeons seem to coo quite differently. They say, 'Take two cows, Daffy. Take two cows, Daffy. Take two cows, Daffy. Do!' The ravens provide the bass part in all choruses.

Sunday, June 2nd

Church was at noon. There is no processional hymn and no procession. The pews are high backed and narrow, with raised seats and I spent my time wondering what would happen if I couldn't get up off my knees in time. The sextoness pumped the organ. She wore a tall hat, and she sat with her wart on her nose plain to all! No one ever thinks of singing the first line of a hymn or a chant, it just isn't done. The minister gave an eloquent sermon with his eyes closed. We had the Morning Prayer, Epistle and Gospel, and then there was a long announcement about Communion next Sunday. All the old ladies ride to the church on bicycles, and today I saw an old man riding a full-grown tricycle.

In the afternoon, Aunt and I drove to Auburn House near Malahide to see Uncle Charlie, his wife Aunt Amos and their two boys, and we enjoyed it immensely. A lovely place, much more settled than Brownstown. The lawn is neater and there is a tennis court and a croquet ground. Large lawn mowers! However, I think Brownstown has better possibilities. The Auburn garden is divided into three by walls with a gate in each. What I liked was the little lookout at the corner of each, with little stone steps overgrown with moss. Between the garden and the house there is a path beside a little fishpond, where we saw tadpoles with newly sprouted legs. Lovely old trees – Uncle Charlie had seven cut down in the meadow in front of the house, and still there are all kinds left.

There is great rivalry between Uncle Charlie and Aunt Olive for gardens. Malahide is about two weeks ahead because it is near the sea. Uncle Charlie has sweet peas in bloom, strawberries ripening, and has new potatoes.

We stayed for supper. We all had salad plates which no one used.

Saturday, June 8th

To Skerries for the afternoon, to visit Grannie. I was absolutely fascinated by the sea at Skerries. No wonder Masefield wrote, 'I must go down to the seas again.' The smell of it, the sound of it, the colour of it, and the white caps further out. The islands offshore are charming, and I felt I could reach out my hand and touch them. The seashore is uncivilized looking, considering the number of holiday people there are every year. It is stony and sandy alternately, and covered with seaweed. I could have sat and watched the sea for hours. I'm just living for the day when I can have a real swim in the real sea.

We then drove to Dublin. We stopped at the Meath Hospital for a few minutes, where Uncle Cyril is a doctor. He showed me the horns of an Irish elk 15,000 to 25,000 years old. The front steps were being fixed and I got on the wrong scaffold and quite annoyed the workmen. It's hard to please everyone.

We stopped for a few moments on Henry Street. Very busy, Saturday shoppers, people walking out in the middle of the street and the cars dodging round them. No one is smartly dressed, and everyone sauntering along as if they had all the time in the world. As H. V. Morton[2] says: 'They have not the haggard money look.'

Sunday, June 9th

Stayed night with Uncle Cyril, at Lower Fitzwilliam Street – Number 15 is one of Morton's Georgian houses, with iron paling outside the windows on the first floor. Early this morning I heard people walking to church. We went to St Ann's at 10 a.m. for Communion, and there was no music until 11:30 a.m. The service is exactly the same as in Canada except for little things – they still say 'Our Father which art ...', no cross on the altar, dim, religious lighting and a very sparse congregation.

The policemen are Celtic looking, talk with a brogue, wear white gloves and handle everything well. Traffic is ridiculous – all the little cars slipping here and there, narrow streets, small trams, and hold-ups by small donkey-carts on the main roads.

Driving home to Brownstown House, about a two hour journey, Aunt and I had a grand time watching for all the milestones along the Dublin

---

2 Author of *In Search of Ireland*, which was often discussed by the family.

Road. I thought such things were legends by this time. Some of them are big and strong, others are crumbling away. A mile according to them is an Irish mile; that is, a mile and a bit, and the bit is longer than the mile! We measured the distance with the dial in the car and an Irish mile[3] is about 1.33 English miles.

Monday, June 10th

Three letters from Calgary. The postman comes just before breakfast, so Aunt and I don't usually do much talking at that meal. The toast usually gets cold.

Went to Knockmark House for tea. I always want to call it Knockmedown! It's a rambling sort of house that used to be the Glebe. All that's left of its church now is a lovely old ivy-covered tower and a few gravestones in the graveyard. Their garden doesn't compare to that at Brownstown, but it has the added attraction of a little brook running through it.

The whole family at Knockmark is hunting mad. Horses, dogs, and hunt meets seem to be their life. The two daughters are marvellous riders, owning fabulous horses. They have elaborate stables, and the best saddles and bridles. Times have been hitting them rather hard lately. They tried having paying guests for a time, and had a bad experience with a young American couple. The damage to the furniture was only just covered by their board bill. They let the bath overflow down the stairs and broke several lamps, among other things. Americans are quite a by-word over here, although everyone says they are charming to meet.

We called in on the neighbours on the way home. I would say he is a typical, Irish gentleman farmer – a good size, very florid, loves a good story or joke, and thinks there is no place like County Meath. He knows everybody's family inside out, from the maiden name of one's great-grandmother to the second name of one's youngest grandson.

I'm getting to know a few birds. Chaffinches fill the garden, and build in the forks of apple trees. Little, grey stonechats build in holes in garden walls, and are extremely wary of entering their nests with people nearby. We often see willy wagtails flying off the road into the hedges. The robin here is a neat little bird, but I think I like our Canadian robin better. I have heard thrushes sing and blackbirds whistle. The blackbirds have very handsome

---

3   An Irish mile was 2,240 yards; a statute mile is 1,760 yards

tails, and a dignified way of walking. They hop across the lawn making a noise like rain to draw out the worms. They love mown grass. Aunt puts crumbs on the window sills for the birds.

The resident cuckoo seems to cuck when everything else is quiet in the evening, or when there is a lull early in the morning. He is getting hoarse now, and sometimes just cucks or just oos. I love the woodpigeon chorus. The rooks congregate in the evening in the trees at the back of the house.

Wednesday, June 12th

Went shopping in Dublin for the first time. Everything seems so slow, and no one seems to be able to find anything. However, I got a crystal for my watch for one shilling. We went into a Kodak shop to leave some films to be developed, and I thought the girl would never get all the bills written out and the numbers added up. She gave us a 'check' with a number on it and when she was tearing it off she tore the number in half. I was in fits.

Went to Trinity College Races. Rather disappointed in lack of enthusiasm displayed – Uncle Charlie said it was an indication that the country was going to the dogs. Events much the same as in Canada, the two mile race being the longest. The various clubs were racing against one another. Pink coats take the place of the blue at Oxford, or Cambridge. They are given as an athletic honour. You don't often see men wearing pink! I rather liked the idea. All Trinity students had green badges. At one end of the park there was a pavilion where all officials and honoured guests sat. The races were announced through a megaphone, and an added attraction was a very good band in the centre of the field.

People seemed to walk round and meet old friends rather than watch the races. I was introduced to a Miss Cunningham, Dean of Women, who said girls were always leaving Trinity Hall, seeking cheaper lodgings. There are about 800 students at Trinity, around a quarter of them are girls, who chiefly take Arts, with some specializing in Modern Languages. Saw the Provost in tails and a tall silk hat. He was passing down the lines lifting his hat, reminding me of the King when he is driving through crowds. Some ladies were dressed up in long flowing robes, frills, gloves and Princess Marina hats, but we felt much more comfortable in our suits than we imagined they did in their flounces. It rained intermittently.

Went through the Engineering School, and I was impressed by the dinginess of the building. The museum was particularly interesting. A mineralogist would have been in his element, as there were samples of every kind of rock and mineral ore. All were in glass cases, and labels told by whom presented. There are several fossils in plaster along the walls, and down the centre of the room is a row of the skeletons of Irish elks about 15,000 years old. They are huge animals, and their age was calculated by dating the deposits of soil in the horns. What most interested me about the collection was the model of the sun, earth, moon, and nearest fixed star set up to scale. At one end of the room is a ball, the size of a pea, to represent the earth; near it is a smaller sphere for the moon, and at the other side of the room (which stretches across the width of the building) is a golden ball, about six inches in diameter, to represent the sun. Out through the window, across the cricket pitch and about four blocks away, is a large building, the roof of which represented the position of the nearest fixed star. I came away feeling like a microbe.

There are some very interesting models of engines. The model of the first steam turbine, invented by a Trinity man, took my fancy. I was also impressed by a model of the Drogheda Viaduct. Down the stairs are photographs of all the Engineer graduates who fell in the Great War.

The antechamber has the queerest floor, with its squares higher along the sides than in the centre. Perhaps the idea is to wake you up for early morning lectures by making you either step easy or fall hard. On one side of the antechamber is a statue of one of the Provosts of about the year 1888. Lecture halls are downstairs, but we didn't intrude into this Holy of Holies.

Friday, June 14th

At night went to the Trinity College Dance at the Metropole. It was the grandest dance I have ever attended, with over 300 there. It was perfect watching from the balcony onto the dance floor – like looking through a kaleidoscope. The floor surface was excellent. So was the orchestra. A great deal of American music was played, and some English pieces. We had a Paul Jones twice, a polka (not like our heel and toe) and several gallops. There were some lovely dresses, and of course, all the men were in tails. It is one of the biggest dances of the year. I was thrilled!

Sunday, June 23rd

Open air service on Tara Hill. I loved it. I had read about Tara Hill, and it seemed romantic to have an open-air service where St Patrick came so long ago. A very good band and one very appropriate hymn: 'O God our help in ages past.' The Bishop of Meath preached, not particularly brilliantly, but acceptably. There were a number of Roman Catholics at the back; they talked all through the prayers and during the sermon, and when the Bishop made an unnecessary remark about Roman Catholics in general, they positively chattered. It was rather uncomfortable. The collection was taken using little bags instead of plates, maybe so that the pound notes wouldn't blow away? There were about three hundred at the service, people from all over Meath, and from Dublin, too. There were hundreds of cars. We went right up on to the hill, beyond the recently built church, to the raths of the church of St Patrick's time. We saw the view stretching out for miles and miles around, all so green, so picturesque, so peaceful.

Thursday, June 27th

Had lunch with friends of the family, at Balrath, just outside Kells, not too far from Brownstown House. They have a beautiful place that was a hospital during the war. The building is bare on the outside, not at all ivy covered; I liked its stark look. There is a courtyard surrounded by stables, a cobblestone driveway, a large clock, and wide steps leading up to the hall door. We knocked and waited. A butler came. When I saw him I was terrified and nearly ran away. Aunt Olive said afterwards she didn't expect him either. She had difficulty in remembering our names for the butler, so that he could announce us as we were ushered into the Oak Room. When we had lunch, a maid followed the butler round as he served us, and then the two of them stood in the room the whole time. I hated that. The butler asked me if I would have some white wine. I thought it was lemonade and said, 'Yes, please.' When I tasted it I was disappointed, but I managed to swallow it. Before I had put the glass down properly, the butler had rushed over and refilled it. I was disgusted and mortified all at once.

Spent the afternoon just looking, hardly speaking. There are about seven gardens, each opening into the next. One could easily get lost. Rockeries, borders, beds, all filled with flowers, some of them very rare specimens. A fruit garden with a huge strawberry bed, and a wall of ripe cherries, about four hundred yards long. They were well screened in to prevent birds being too greedy. A jay thrush had got in while we were there, so we let him loose. He was just a baby, terribly frightened, screaming like nothing on earth or in heaven. There are about seven hot houses in another garden. One of them had ripe figs; that was the first time I had eaten such a thing. Another was the vine hot house, with many bunches of green grapes. Peaches and pears in yet another. The begonia and geranium hothouse gave the most beautiful display I have ever seen. Begonias the size of large mums in the deepest of yellows, reds, and oranges. There were six under-gardeners and one head gardener. The head gardener's house is what Canadians would consider very grand.

There are twenty-five boxes for horses in the stables, and two hounds for hunting, handsome looking dogs full of life. The deer park is real, with about fifty deer and twenty fawns. I tried to photograph them, but they were too timid and I was too slow.

The house is a mansion. There is a vast hall from one end to the other where the grandfather used to pace up and down for exercise when for some political reason it wasn't safe to go out. The Oak Room is a marvel. All the walls are solid oak with carved figures on them, some Italian, others English. Set on a carved desk in one corner is a pair of high, carved candlesticks.

The library is immense and I was longing to have a good look at the books. The room has a billiard table and ping-pong table, and steps are being made out of the window in one corner on to the tennis court at the back.

The house is full of old paintings, many of them Italian in character and quite immodest. Just as you come in through the door into the hall there are two life-size, nude statues. Our hostess said she was going to make them some winter clothes.

Monday, July 1st

This being Canada Day, it seems strange not to have a holiday with fireworks and elaborate celebrations. Wondering how Bowness Park at home is faring with its double fare, hourly cars, and 50¢ canoe rides. Quiet day here at Brownstown, picking red currants and peas, and making haycocks for the men. Played croquet in the afternoon, walked around the estate with the dogs in the evening.

Wednesday, July 3rd

Aunt and I went down to the hayfield and drove the horse and rake. I was frightened at first because the mare is so efficient and I was just the opposite, but after I had been round a few times and messed a few rows of hay about, it came more easily. It's the thrill that comes once in a lifetime to realize that you are the brains of a machine like that! I was warned against letting the

47

lever fly back and hit my elbow. It did, of course. In this case, once bitten always shy; it hasn't happened since. We were told afterwards we had been of great assistance – Aunt certainly was, she took to it with ease.

It was market day and Aunt Olive and I drove in and sat watching the men bidding. They slap each other's hands as they bid, often spitting on their own hands first to make the slap more effective. The bidders usually wear brown coats and the sellers always carry a stick, a useful implement to keep the cattle together. And the voices! I never heard such harsh tones, it is like some sort of a foreign language. One particular man was abusing a bidder who was much too low to suit him, but we couldn't understand it all. The street was a filthy sight with cattle standing all over the sidewalks and on people's front doorsteps, making messes, and the men waving their sticks frantically at any errant animal.

After supper we went out to the little graveyard behind Brownstown House, where people have been buried for at least two hundred years, and where there used to be a little church. A few of the ruined walls still stand and the remains of an old vault are visible. The caretaker was at one end cutting down the long grass with a scythe. When he saw us he gave a little jump and then said, 'I thought you was somebody got up'. Then he told us very proudly that he stayed there until eleven o'clock at night, when it is still almost daylight here, and it never worried him at all. People round here think he should get the VC for bravery. He said that one gravestone, dated 1786, 'had a very old perscription'. I squeezed Aunt's arm, but managed to keep a straight face. The Irish never say *it's* or *it is*, but always *'tis*. We surprised a fox, and it ran across my feet and away to the fields.

Saturday, September 7th

Various gypsies come to the house asking for help. One man who was given a lot of apples last year (apples from the tree that bore 2,458 apples in one summer) came back again the other day and asked for some bread and butter. This he was given, but still he lingered on, hemming and hawing, until he finally picked up courage and asked, 'Have you e'er an apple, Ma'am?' A gypsy woman asked for some shoes last Spring, and she was told that the only shoes she could have were the ones on Aunt's feet, and there was a lot of wear in them still. She reappeared the other day and asked again for the shoes. Aunt said that she took them off very reluctantly and handed them over. The woman sat down on the wet doorstep to put them on. 'Be careful,' warned Aunt Olive, 'That step is wet'. 'I often sits in wetter places' was the reply. The shoes wouldn't begin to go on, as her stocking had no foot, her foot was bound up with rags, and was the size of a mountain. She took the shoes anyway, and Aunt said she very sadly watched her going off, carrying the respectable gardening shoes. To whom would they ever be sold?

Wednesday, September 11th

Went to town, had prawns on toast at Roberts Café. Went over to Trinity to make enquiries about the possibility of my studying there, at Uncle Cyril's suggestion. There is talk of Uncle Cyril offering to pay my fees. Saw Mr Russell, the Bursar. It is all so different from Calgary, no system, no method, no rhyme or reason, and half the time you don't know whether the man is making jokes or talking business. A pair of slippers over beside the fireplace, a coat in another corner with an umbrella on top of it, a telephone just over one of the chairs so that every time the 'phone rang I had to get up. A man came in about some receipts, the files had to be found, and after a lot of searching, Mr Russell said the man was plain stupid and must have sent receipts to the wrong person. It was all so informal. The subject came up as to whether or not most people were honest. 'Well,' said Mr Russell, 'I believe in trusting a man, but I do think most of us have a little natural ability to be dishonest.' The Registrar is away. 'For how long?' we asked. 'Pay day is on Thursday', was the reply.

Saw a collie trained to run under a cart at the horse's heels. Apparently they run like that for miles and never get hurt. It must be hard to train them.

Sunday, October 6th

Learnt how to fold table napkins the smart way, and how to make tomato sandwiches! I needed to learn because my sandwiches got soggy and crumbled, so much so that the maid declined to put them on the tea table. Aunt and I had them in private for supper. To think I can't make a sandwich when I have made a school lunch in three minutes. Laugh!

Friday, October 11th (on the Mailboat going across the Irish Sea, en route to Canada, via Liverpool and London)

Caught the Irish Mail from the Dun Laoghaire pier. It was a good crossing.

The sea was as calm as a mill pond. The boat moves from back to front, the seagulls flew after the boat, some following us the whole way across. Ireland looked beautiful, disappearing. Old country houses have such straight fronts, they are built in such blocks, that they give a very unique appearance to a harbour. The Dublin Mountains were lovely as a background for it all. I already miss the Irish humour and the twinkle of the eye.

7

HOME TO CALGARY 1935–37

I arrived back home from my trip to Ireland, but I didn't know what I was going to do. Eventually, I took a business course, typing and shorthand, in which I did not excel. I managed to type very fast, but I also made a lot of errors. Shorthand wasn't so bad, I quite liked it, but I've never really used it at all. I do type well enough now. I didn't like the man in the school that I went to. He was a pill.

It was rather miserable in Calgary after being in Ireland, because I couldn't get a job. The Depression was still on, quite severely. There were no jobs. I did eventually sell stationery and books for the Hudson's Bay Company. But we weren't allowed to look inside a book. I had to stand there; it was a long day and I got $12.10 per week. I was part-time. They were very mean, bringing me in at 12 noon, which meant I had to leave home at 11, coming in without lunch. They gave me no break. I worked to 6, but I had to stay and clean up the place. So that meant I didn't get the streetcar until 7. I wasn't home until 8.

The only thing that I liked was that most of the staff in the department were very interesting, two university graduates and one artist, and there was a pleasant atmosphere. We had a bit of a bumbling boss, but we tolerated him and quite liked him. Then they asked me if I would go up to the advertising place and work there. Although I was very honoured to be asked, it would not have been a good thing for me, having to think up slogans, write advertisements, do a lot of typing. I could type well, but I think I would have been unhappy up there.

I don't have a lot of respect for the Hudson's Bay Company as a result of my time with them. But I learned some good things. I saw a lot of what went on. They would have a nine-cent-day about every three months, and we would put all the usual stationery and any other knick-knacks that we sold there out of sight, and we would bring down inferior stuff from the attic in big boxes. Nine cents for each item bought.

My father was a great man for asking to see the manager if something didn't suit him. While I was still there on the staff, he went in and bought a shirt which didn't suit him. There was something wrong with it, which he considered was not his fault. So he went back and he asked to see the manager. Eventually the manager came down and provided him with another shirt. I didn't know all this, and I would have been horrified had I known at the time.

I was glad I was in the book department. I used to take the books home. I could read them in the streetcar, and I read *Gone with the Wind* that way. We had to bring it back the next day, as someone might buy it. I always remember one customer who used to come in regularly. She was a gentle creature, and she always had candies with her, and she would give each of us one. It was a personal thing. She'd make a beeline for us in the book department when she came into the shop. We used to think, 'Well, that is a nice one!' But some of the customers were dreadful. Some of them were married and with small children. They would come in and throw their weight around. It was quite an experience. It didn't do me any harm, but if I had been at it much longer it would have. We used to stand in a row, sometimes, 'presenting a front to the enemy,' the manager told us.

I was bored, and fortunately it didn't last. But I didn't know where I was going, or what kind of a future I would have. Entries from my diary for this period illustrate my concerns.

Friday, April 23rd, 1937

Inspection day at The Bay. Such a busy department we were, polishing, tidying, rearranging, and scrubbing, all to the tune of 'Let's Hurry'. A squabble over where to place magazines heated until the atmosphere was cleared by sudden laughter. Three inspectors appeared three times, all followed by a lazy lot of girls this afternoon, reading books and magazines and going on 'buying trips'. Heavy, wet snow is weighing down the trees outside. Arriving home I discovered the wind's strength and direction had forced the flying snow under the roof rafters. Snow is piled high in the corner of my bedroom, and all over Hugh's and Brian's bed. What a mess!

Monday, June 7th, 1937

My 21st birthday. Spoke to no-one about it being my birthday. Rode home on my bike after work, with my spiked heels, bare knees and my things in a large cotton bundle tied on with a fuzzy brown rope dotted with oil. Road home is bumpy, in the thick of zooming cars, loose stones and disgruntled thoughts. The bundle came untied once, fell off the bike twice and the rain began to come. My legs were tired, as I rode through torrents of rain, reaching home totally soaked. Sat down to a supper of turnips, bacon and eggs, reading the paper and listening to thoughtless kids tap dancing in the next room. Suddenly the door opened to 'Come here, right away!' I was led out to the hall to a chorus of 'Surprise! Happy Birthday!' It was sweet.

Knowing that I would manage the household for her, my mother went over to Ireland alone to visit all her relatives in 1936. A photograph of our family had been taken in Calgary. Mother had sent copies to her brothers in Ireland, who had been so shocked by her white hair and worn out appearance, that they sent her the return fare to Dublin. They took her on a tour around the southwest of Ireland, which she had always longed to see. She received a renewal of the offer my Uncle Cyril, her brother, had made in 1935, to pay my fees to go to Trinity. When I heard this news, I cried for joy, because I knew it would come true, this time.

In 1935, my father had objected to the offer, and had instructed me to return home. He had a very keen sense of the fact that if you emigrate to a country you should make your home and your life there. You should not try to live on two sides of the Atlantic. He felt that that was what would happen to me, as indeed it has. I always feel trans-Atlantic. My father also said that no daughter of his was going to receive charity from his wife's brother. But, for me, it made no sense not to get the university education I wanted when there was no hope of getting it any other way. So I just said that I was going, and he didn't say anything this time. I was 21. I think he finally realised the kind of life I was having in Calgary, with no prospects, and not many friends. I hadn't got a university degree, and what was I going to do? I could have gone into what they call 'Normal School', which taught you to be a teacher, particularly for junior forms, and though I was interested in teaching, I was much more intent on getting a university degree. I had considered being a nurse, but Dad very wisely said that he didn't think I was the kind of person who should be shut in with sick people. I acquiesced in that, but I didn't acquiesce in the idea I should not be able to go to Trinity.

When I was invited to come to Trinity, I had been in the Hudson's Bay Company for about eight months. I had saved a bit of money so I was able to buy a few clothes for myself before I went over to Trinity College Dublin.

I never saw my father again. I left Calgary for the final time in 1937, and he died in 1941, in January. I had written home every week, but I hadn't been able to get home because of the War.

8

UNDERGRADUATE AT TRINITY COLLEGE DUBLIN 1937–40

Sailing from Canada in the autumn of 1937, I landed in Liverpool where I spent the night with an old friend and distant relative of my mother, in Liverpool 8. I believe that area, which was Georgian houses, or certainly very tall Victorian houses, became quite a slum afterwards. But this was before the war, and I remember looking out, down the street. It was so high! I had never slept in anything like that before. My hostess knew a young ordinand and she asked him to take me round Liverpool Cathedral, which was still in a state of being built. It took a long time to build that Cathedral, and he was knowledgeable about it. He showed me the window that Giles Scott put in, in memory of his mother. A very small window. He talked about 'the flicks' and I had no idea what he meant. He took me to a movie, but I had never heard movies called 'the flicks' before. Then I took the night boat from Liverpool to Dublin. There my mother's brother, Uncle Cyril, in whose house I was going to stay, met me, and he took me to where he lived, 15 Lower Fitzwilliam Street. He was living with his mother, my grandmother, who was about 81 at the time and in a wheelchair. She lived longer than any of the family, but she didn't live long after I arrived.

It was like fairyland to me, going to Dublin and then going to Trinity but it wasn't straightforward, trying to arrange about my courses. For one thing, I had done two years at the University of Alberta, and Trinity had never recognised that University. It didn't exist as far as they were concerned. There was a Board meeting, and the Board had to vet the fact that it was a proper university. Then they gave me credit for one year, which I think was fair enough. So, I came into Trinity as a Senior Freshman. It was probably as much as I could manage. There was quite a lot to do as it was. My father, who was a Trinity graduate, thought my coming in from a different educational system would be a strain. He advised me to register for a Pass Degree in French, English and, I think, Chemistry. Three courses. But I didn't stay with it for long.

I found the people I was sitting in lectures with were so silly. I suppose they were immature. I was 21, older than most students, and I didn't warm to this particular lot. When I went in to No. 6, the gathering place for women attending the university, I would see all kinds of people who weren't a bit like the people in the Pass class. I thought about it a long time. My tutor was Harry Thrift, and I don't know how much he was interested in me or what I was doing. But I had to go to him and say that I wanted to do Honours. Meanwhile, I was told I should probably do the Pass exam to be held just after Christmas, at the end of the holiday. I went to ask Mrs Godfrey, who was the Lady Registrar, about it, and she said, 'Well, I can understand that perhaps you wouldn't want to do Pass, but what you really need is a very easy course. I recommend you do History.' I remember telling Dr Moody about this long afterwards and he was furious! But, he wasn't there at the time. It was still Professor Phillips who was Professor of History. I also remember that for my last exam in Canada I was doing five subjects, quite advanced Chemistry, English, French, Maths and History. I got the best mark in History for the least effort, so I thought, 'I've got to get through this course in Trinity, two years and two terms. What I'd better do is pass it.' And so the idea of History, for many reasons, appealed to me. I was never sorry I had gone to it.

Immediately after I got into that course, I began to find some interesting friends. One of them, one of the Gwynns, I still know now. She lives in England and I correspond with her. It was such a relief, really. The recommended books were so interesting, the lecturers were more interesting. The youngest, least experienced lecturers taught the Pass courses.

When I was arranging for my papers to be accepted after the university credits had been recognised, there was no mention of one of the subjects that was supposed to be essential for entrance; geometry, I think it was. Captain Shaw was working in the Senior Lecturer's office, he knew some of my relations, and he was very kind and took quite an interest in me. He went upstairs to see the Senior Lecturer, a man called Matty Fry. He got my papers accepted, even though he knew they were somewhat deficient. When Captain Shaw came down, I asked, 'How did you manage that?' 'Shhh!' he said. There was no geometry on it. I wasn't worried because I wasn't going on in Mathematics, anyway. But eventually I had to do it in Little-go, the Final Freshman examination.

So I got myself settled. Then I had to pay my fees, for which my uncle gave me the cheque. I remember going in to the Bursar's office where there was a secretary. The Bursar was Russell, and he had his shoes heating by the fire. The whole place was heated by a fire, there was no question of central heating at that time. He had his slippers on, and I thought that was very nice, that you paid your fees to a man who was wearing his slippers. He was rather a pet, I thought. But his secretary sat there, glowering at me and eventually she shouted, 'Take your hat off!' Everybody wore a hat at the time. I used to keep out of her way after that. That was one of my early experiences.

I used to love walking out onto the streets of Dublin, going along Wicklow Street, or up Grafton Street, smelling all those lovely smells. I thought Dublin was a most delightful city. The smell of coffee dominated Grafton Street. There is still a Bewley's in Grafton Street, but I don't notice those smells now. I was housekeeping for Uncle Cyril, and I got to know shops like Leverett and Frye. There were no supermarkets, so I had to go from shop to shop, carrying the purchases. In Canada, you would go to one shop, and they always delivered the goods for you. Now, I had to carry the food all the way back to Fitzwilliam Street, but I didn't mind. I was at University at last, to which I had wanted to go for three years, and for which I had not had the slightest hope. It was a very happy time.

I had quite a lot of social life with my family, my mother's people, here. Their children were younger than I was, but still, it was very nice to have them about. And I was still busy housekeeping. There were two maids, but I had to plan the meals.

My grandmother also lived with Uncle Cyril, and she got on with some very good maids. She used to write to convents. There was a special convent in Ballinasloe with which she had contact. She would write enquiring for a maid, and she would sign herself 'Emma Murphy', which was her name. The nuns and the Mother Superior in the convents thought she was a good Catholic, with that name. They didn't worry about sending their girls to her. When I was married and the maid market was very shaky, and hardly any maids could be

57

found anywhere, I tried the convent, like my grandmother. But of course my name was wrong, and they would write and say, 'Would she have time for her spiritual duties?' Eventually, when I said that we were Protestants, the Mother Superior wrote and said she was sorry, the girls couldn't manage to come up to Dublin. So I gave up.

The cook my grandmother had had in the house stayed on for quite a while after Grannie died, when I was housekeeping. My grandmother used to talk to her, and ask her about her day off: 'What had happened?' and 'Whom did she meet?' My grandmother was in a wheelchair by this time, so she was very glad to have a little chat with Annie. 'Where did you go, Annie?' 'Oh,' said Annie, 'I was sheltering under a tree, and a priest came up, and we began to talk, because it was raining hard and we were standing there a long time, and he asked me what I was doing, and I said I was with a very nice family, a cook general.' 'I hope good Catholics,' said the priest. 'Indeed, no,' said Annie, '*they* don't know how to treat you!' Annie went for her day off with a Garda Síochána, a policeman she was walking out with at the time. My grandmother asked her, 'Where did you go?' Annie told her where she had gone walking and where she had taken her tea. Annie didn't seem to mind these questions, and eventually my grandmother said, 'You must get tired walking around, Annie. Don't you ever sit down?' 'Oh, Ma'am,' she said, 'If you sat down you'd be destroyed.' That reply is still a family saying. If I'm tired and people say, 'Go and sit down!' I say 'I'm better to keep up because if I sat down I'd be destroyed!' In other words, I'd fall asleep.

It was a bit of a struggle to try to keep up what you thought were 'standards', and a doctor had to have his door opened by somebody in a cap and apron. You had to be ready, by two o'clock, for the first patient. The maids lived down in the basement. That was quite a good house, the basement was all right. But it was a bit dreary to be in the basement. There were two maids and they got on together very well. They used to talk to each other. My uncle was within earshot one day when my grandmother rang her bell. She needed something. My uncle heard one maid say to the other, 'I wonder what Emma wants now?' But they were entirely demure and respectful anytime they came upstairs.

Annie was delighted any time Archdeacon Crozier came to visit. He had archdeacon clothes on, wearing gaiters in those days, and he was a very handsome man. Annie used to announce him. She'd throw open the door into the sitting room where my grandmother was sitting. 'Mr Archdeacon!' she would say. She knew exactly how to do it. After he left one time, Annie was getting my grandmother her lunch and Annie said, 'Oh, that's a lovely man. He's the image of my Guard!'

We lit the fires only in the afternoon, after lunch. Uncle Cyril had a fire in his consulting room ready for his patients a little earlier than that. I didn't know how to light fires. I suspect some of those maids we had didn't know how to set them either. It took me ages to get a fire going. I would work at a table and chair set up near the fire, trying to keep myself warm. I used to shiver in the house, and I had chilblains on my hands and my feet. It was pretty cold. I didn't always go back to College in the afternoon. Fitzwilliam Street to Trinity isn't very far; it took perhaps fifteen minutes walking. I think the kitchen, which was downstairs, had an Aga cooker. At that time, a lot of people did get Agas, which were absolute bliss, until they ran out of anthracite during the War. Then, they had to shut down the stove because they couldn't get any anthracite. In the evenings, there were no electric blankets to warm the beds. That was the time of day it was even colder. Dublin was a foggy city in those days, and the fog used to come right in through the window.

Before that first term was over, my grandmother became quite ill. She was allergic to various things. Uncle Cyril was one of the early doctors interested in allergies. He discovered Grannie was quite seriously allergic to feathers. She did eventually die of asthma. Other people have said my grandmother had a bad heart, which no doubt she had. But I remember my uncle saying to his brother, who was also a doctor, 'Mother died out of her lungs.' Grandmother died a week before Christmas, and all the relatives came. It was quite an upheaval in the family. We all went down to the country, and there was a big funeral.

There was a man who had lived in the gate lodge of Rathcore Rectory, where my grandmother and grandfather had lived, and where their children were born. He heard my grandmother was not well, up in Dublin. He somehow hired some kind of a taxi, and he came up to see her. It was very moving to see him, as he could hardly walk himself. I think Grannie had been a very good Rector's wife. She had medical sense. All her family seemed to have. Her brother became a distinguished doctor in Dublin, and in the next generation, my mother's four brothers and one sister became doctors. It was a record in the British Isles at the time.

I had never been so close to death before, and it all happened at home. It was quite an experience. My aunts and uncles said that I had been so disturbed for the last three weeks of term, that they thought they should get me some grinds for my exams, especially in Mathematics. Although I had been fairly good at Mathematics when I was at school, it was quite obvious that I wasn't going to get any better at it. It wasn't my thing. So I went to a grinder called John Hutton, who lived in Waterloo Place. He was a nephew of Glen Hutton, the famous cricketer. This Mr Hutton persisted in saying, 'Play *The Maple Leaf.* I'd like to hear you play *The Maple Leaf.'* Well, I didn't really play the piano, so I disappointed him. But I got through the exams, and that was the main thing.

Having passed the exam, I was then free to go into the History school. There was an exam in History by Easter, so I had to work very hard. Also, Little-go was coming up at the end of the academic year, but I concentrated on the History first. I never seemed to be told anything. Harry Thrift never told me, and I didn't go and ask him what times the exams started. Instead, I looked at the list of exams at Front Gate, showing subjects and dates. I looked for the time of the exam, and it was 10, in brackets. So I turned up at 10 o'clock on the day and Miss Griffith came up to me because she was invigilating the exam. She said, 'Why are you so late?' I replied, 'I followed the instructions at Front Gate. There it says 10 o'clock.' 'Oh,' she said. So when 12:30 came, time for the exam to be over, I asked if I could possibly have some extra time. 'You're fortunate I take your paper at all', she said. 'I would like to see where you got this false information.' So I took her to the Front Gate and I showed her. 'Oh, that 10 just means there were ten pupils up for the exam.' However, I did manage to pass. I got a 'second', I think. Meanwhile, Harry Thrift became a Senior Fellow, and gave up being a tutor. So I moved on. Several people said I should go to Mr Godfrey, that he was the best. So I did what was suggested. Godfrey told me, 'You know, with what you have had to cope with, that's a very good result. Go on, and you'll be all right.' That was encouraging.

Next, I had to pass Little-go. I started to do some lectures in pass Latin, and in Chemistry, which I chose because I had done quite a lot of Chemistry in Canada. I didn't do Physics, or Mechanics. I didn't know anything about them at all. I worked the whole summer, without a holiday. And I made up the Latin. Six books of Virgil. I had done lower level Latin in Canada. I had taken enough to know what I had to do to get through, and I had a dictionary, and I worked hard at it. I liked Virgil. I thought it was a pity to have to translate it into English, it sounded so well in Latin.

Little-go came in the Autumn. I had to do a History exam, as well, because one had to do an exam every term in your subject when I was there. I managed to improve my History mark. Then I went on and did Little-go. Meanwhile,

Mr Godfrey suggested I try the Scholarship the next year, but I had to put that out of my mind while I was doing Little-go. I had mixed success with Little-go. Unfortunately, it didn't include History at all. Anyone I knew who was doing Science, or doing a Language, had a boost, one study session for two exams, but I did manage somehow to cope.

There was one bit of good luck in the exam, and one bit of bad luck. They had so many students, they had to use halls other than the Exam Hall for them, and they put me in the Dining Hall. The bad luck was that 'W' generally got the worst places in the Dining Hall. And it was the tradition of the College that the Provost, with the Senior Fellows, walked through every hall during Little-go. The Provost was W. E. Thrift, a small man. I can still see him. And they came into the Dining Hall. 'Pray stand for the Provost!' said the Porter at the door. So we all stood up. And I had just seen my way through a Geometry problem, which I was fairly good at, but which I didn't find easy. And by the time I had seen the parade going by and had sat down again, the solution had gone from me. We had only an hour and a half, which wasn't very long, and I failed the exam.

Fortunately, when we came to Latin, I got Bedell Stanford for the oral. Two of us were up for the oral together. I think it was Leslie Tyrrell with me – Ty… and Wa… aren't too far apart. And Bedell Stanford looked at me. I was absolutely stuck. Eventually he said, 'Would you rather have another piece?' So I said, 'Yes, please!' He gave me another piece, and I knew that one. And I got 6, which isn't a brilliant mark, but it was all right for me. If I had failed Latin as well as the Geometry, I would have had to do Little-go again, after Christmas. You could fail one exam, but you weren't allowed to fail two. A long time afterwards, I said to Bedell Stanford, 'You were a kind examiner!' And I reminded him of what had happened. He said, 'You know, just occasionally I get a feeling about somebody, but it's very rare that I give them a second choice.'

Meanwhile, I got the Geometry in the 're-ex', as they called it, but it took a lot of my time. It disturbed my term, really. However, I went on, and I worked very hard over the Christmas break. I was in a special position, and I had to get through. I didn't take much time off, working seven and eight hours a day. I did the History exam after Christmas, which I enjoyed. I got a slightly better mark. Then, Mr Godfrey again said, 'I think you should try the Scholarship.' My chief difficulty was I had practically no knowledge of Irish History, which was a paper in itself. I spent a long time with Professor Curtis' book on Irish History, which was good factually, but his style, I thought, was terrible. Eventually, I managed to get some sense from it. The English History I had done before, and some European, so that wasn't quite so bad. Meanwhile, I was getting to know a few people, which I found very pleasant. I joined the Elizabethan Society, and went to their debates, meeting a few more people there. But I was very much of a workaholic at the time.

Based somewhat on my results in the Christmas examinations, I decided that I would go in for Scholarship, or Schol as it is known to this day. I worked very solidly until the month that Schol came, which was April. To prepare, I had part of January, all of February and March, and part of April. It was somewhat complicated by the fact that I was housekeeping for Uncle Cyril. Aunt Olive, with whom I had stayed in Brownstown House, and who was now remarried to John Hallowes, was pregnant with their son, Geordie. Aunt Olive Hallowes stayed in Uncle Cyril's house, because her home was down in the country, about 40 miles away. She could not risk going into labour down there, and having to be driven that distance up to Dublin to the Nursing Home where the baby was to be born. I used to have to take her out for a walk. She didn't like going out for walks on her own, and yet she had to go for exercise. We used to wait sometimes until it was dark, as she said she felt happier about going at that time, for she really was very ungainly. It cut into my work for Scholarship, for my mind was on her. One amusing episode occurred when we were walking along the canal one evening, in March. A couple of fellows approached us, and said, not knowing what they were talking about, 'Two fine girls!' We used that expression for quite a long time afterwards.

There weren't any other interruptions, and I didn't tell my family back home in Canada that I was doing Schol because I was so sure I wouldn't get it. I didn't want to raise their hopes at all. And apparently my letters home were very thin – no wonder, I was doing nothing but work at the time. My mother was quite worried about what I was concealing.

At that time, 1939, Schol results were not announced for nearly six weeks after the exams. Trinity Monday was announcement day, and it was very much the Trinity Monday according to the Church calendar. No announcement was made until that day. Nor was anyone warned to be there or not to be there. Nowadays they do tell you. They say, 'It would be better for you to be in Front Square on Trinity Monday.' It was pretty much of a strain for everyone, going in there with all kinds of people standing around. There were two in my year that didn't get it, and they were very upset. I thought it was dreadful they had to stand there and hear the other names read out. I thought I'd be one of those left standing. My aunt by marriage, Vera Murphy, told me she was coming in to Front Square to hear the announcements. If I had been a little bit shrewder I would have realised she wouldn't be coming in unless she thought that there was quite a good chance I got it. She was the daughter of the Vice-Provost, so if I had put my thinking cap on, I would have known that she probably knew whether I had got it or not. He would have told her. But she was not in a position to tell me.

There was one student, two years ahead of me, who used to make snide remarks. He had got a scholarship himself. He used to make comments about some people a year before me getting a scholarship. He didn't think they were worthy of it. And I remember perfectly well saying, after my name had been read out as receiving a scholarship, 'I suppose that same fellow will have a lot to say about me today.' Right then, somebody gave me a push, and there he was, right behind me. However, Vice-Provost Goligher came down and chatted to me for a while. It was all exciting and all such a surprise.

Getting Schol happened at a very good time for me because Uncle Cyril, with whom I had been living, had just got engaged, and was about to get married. I was still staying in the house, and he asked me to stay on with them. But it would have been a bad arrangement, especially for the new bride. Another uncle in the Air Force came over from England to visit, bringing his wife. She was quite clear that I should not be there, in the house. So in 1939 they paid for me to go to Trinity Hall, the residence for women attending Trinity. It was a big break in my time in College. I got to know even more people and I got into the atmosphere in College in a better way than I ever could have while living at my uncle's house. I made some good friends at Trinity Hall, including Betty Harman and Doris Wilson.

It had been quite easy to walk to College from Lower Fitzwilliam Street. I didn't have any bus fares to cope with, or anything like that, at that time. It was different when I got to Trinity Hall. We found out that if we walked down to Frankfurt Avenue, which took about 10 minutes, and took the tram from there to the top of Grafton Street instead of staying on and winding round Dawson Street to get closer to Trinity, it cost us only one penny. If we caught the tram right at Trinity Hall, and stayed on until we got all the way to College, then it was three pence. So it was rather nice to save two pennies every time, and each way. Then I got a bicycle in the spring, and I used to ride to Trinity. It was quicker, but I could get soaked going along, with the weather quite often blowing against me.

Miss Cunningham was Warden in Trinity Hall. This was her last year. She had held that position at the time when Aunt Geraldine, a younger sister of my mother's and who was my medical aunt, had gone through College with the second group of women doctors, qualifying in 1915. She had been in Trinity Hall for the first year of Miss Cunningham's time as Warden there. Trinity Hall had just been opened as a Hostel for women students. Miss Cunningham remembered my Aunt Geraldine, and she particularly remembered the crowd she was with. 'Yes,' said Miss Cunningham, 'I can hear voices all day long. Everywhere I go in this building I hear voices.'

They were a distinguished group of women. You had to be exceptionally bright to get into College in those days. And you had to be academic even to want to go, because it was so unusual for a woman to go to University. Either you were thought to be a freak, or you were thought to be a blue-stocking, which was another kind of oddity. But they had a very good time among themselves, these women. And they had a wonderful social life. Aunt Geraldine was well-known for arriving to write her medical exams wearing a full-length evening gown, having been out dancing all night long the night before the exam. I suppose there were about twenty of them. They called themselves 'The Family', and each had a place in it. One was Mother, another Father, and so on.

Maria Jordan was one of that Family. She married Dean Wilson, a very famous Dean of St Patrick's, who was very musical. Aunt Geraldine was asked to be bridesmaid, but she couldn't be bridesmaid because she couldn't afford to buy the material for the dress. She would have made it herself, but the cost of the material was too high. On the day of her wedding, Maria Jordan came to see Aunt Geraldine, gave her a little gift and said she was so sorry she wasn't being a bridesmaid.

Getting Schol made a great difference to my finances, but they didn't give you anything off your Trinity Hall accommodation expenses. I was called a 'Non-Foundation Scholar', which meant that I didn't get rooms in College. Well, no women lived in College, anyway. But, they could have paid for something towards your fees in Trinity Hall, or even given you a little extra pocket money. That would have been the best part, as far as I was concerned. However, I didn't want for anything, really. I lived frugally, but I was pretty hard up. Uncle Cyril had been so generous with me up to then. My family couldn't afford to send me money from Canada. There were four more children coming along. Then my father became ill. He had a stroke. There was no question of my asking for money from them.

In those days you couldn't get a job in the summer. The one job I did manage to get was tutoring two children. They had come over from England, and would not be settled into a school for another two months. The parents thought they should be tutored. They were nice children. Their father, Mr Bradbury made stockings. I used to go out by tram from Trinity Hall to Monkstown, and teach them for three or four hours, three mornings a week. It was all quite strenuous. But, I thought, 'Well, now, if I get enough money I could get my fare back to Canada, when my courses are over.' Originally, I had come over to see how I would get on for a year. Of course, by the time I was finished it was 1940, travel was not possible with the War. There was no question of getting back to Canada. But I did have a little nest egg when I graduated. The Bradburys were very nice to me, very good employers, and I taught the children in the Salthill Hotel in Monkstown. Tea, or sometimes coffee, was brought up in the middle of the session, and I liked the two girls. They were lively and anxious to learn.

Getting Schol also made me consider going on and doing some research in History, which I hadn't thought of before. There would be some small financial backing for me. There was some assistance, £40 a year seems to be in my head, and I did go on, in fact, after I got Moderatorship, or Mod as it was called, in 1940. But that was a year later. Meanwhile, I did the course, instead of in four years, in two years and two terms. Again, the Irish History was strange to me. I'd heard of the Pale, and I knew there'd been fights between the British and the Irish, but I didn't know much more than that. So I didn't go away on any holidays. I had to study.

Even when I was at Trinity Hall, I used to try to attend Church with Uncle Cyril, who was Church Warden in St Ann's in Dawson Street. It was difficult to get there from Trinity Hall for the 10 o'clock service, because the trams didn't run on Sundays. Occasionally I attended Church in Temple Road, near Trinity Hall. Resident men had to go to Chapel in Trinity. They would be checked up on. I remember hearing one man called Norman, one of the students, saying that the Junior Dean, who was Kenneth Bailey at the time, arrived at his door. He hadn't been to Chapel the previous Sunday, so he thought he was going to get ticked off. But the Junior Dean said to Harold Norman, 'I'm not here on official business.' Norman replied, 'Then you are welcome, Sir.'

You went to lectures in a gown. They were compulsory, and if you went to a lecture without one, you were called 'naked!' They were silly little things – a piece of material down the back, elaborate holes for your arms to go through, a little bit of material in the front, and a tassel here and there. There were stories of people being turned out of lectures because they didn't wear a gown. You could buy gowns second-hand.

There was no central heating, and few fires. By 1940, coal was getting a bit scarce. The rooms were very cold – I had constant chilblains. The cold got even worse after the war, in the winter of 1946/47, when there was no coal at all, only a bit of wet turf. Each student used to bring in a sod of turf to try to build up a fire. My husband said, when he was lecturing, his students were all little hooded creatures, with some kind of material covering their hands, and their hand shaking while they took notes. He could just see the hand coming out, because it was so very cold. That was a terrible winter.

I did have lunch in Trinity, perhaps when there was a meeting. Many meetings were held in the afternoon at that time, which helped women, of course. I was quite involved with the History Society, and if there was a meeting on, I would tend to have lunch, which wasn't very appetising. Lunch was provided in No. 6. It would be on a plate. There would be a sandwich, and sometimes there was a bit of cold meat. They didn't cover them over. By the time we had lectures, the lunch had dried out. Classics students had lectures from 1 p.m. to 2 p.m., which was worse. The girls in Classics would rush in early, pick out a certain amount of food, put it away in a special place, covered, so that they could have it when they came in after 2 o'clock. That way, they knew there would be something left.

Overall, the lunches were rather bad, but it was good for meeting people you wouldn't have lectures with, which I found very helpful and very pleasant. I got to know Joyce McGilligan at that time. She was Mod. Lang. and very much into Players, the drama group. We became very good friends after Trinity, and our friendship lasted for the rest of our lives. I was made librarian of the History Library, which was quite a Library. There was some awful old stuff in there, which we eventually got rid of. I found it all quite interesting. I found a list of people, borrowers who hadn't returned books, and I sent all these people notices. Unaccustomed to having to return books, they turned up, baffled. 'What was the History Society coming to?' they asked.

Some of the lectures given to the society were very good. One talk I greatly regret not having made notes of, but it was my early times in Trinity. It was given by Professor Alison Phillips, who was the Lecky Professor of Modern History. He retired in 1939, and sometime during 1938–39 he was persuaded to come and talk to us about his roots. Very interesting. He would never live in Ireland. He commuted entirely. His wife didn't live in Ireland. Occasionally she came over, because my Aunt Vera knew her. But they were based in England. He would come for seven weeks, for term time, when they would live apart. At the end of seven weeks, he would leave the country. So the Board was very determined when it came time for Phillips' successor to be appointed, that one of the conditions must be that Professors of History live here.

Professor Phillips claimed he lived here, which wasn't true, but he was half an actor. I was very sorry that I missed his lectures on the French Revolution, because he used to act it out, from one side, left side to the right, then right side to the left, and the students said he was marvellous. But the year I had him must have been his final year, and although he was a good lecturer he wasn't into this dramatic technique anymore. After he retired, that would be in the summer before my last year, he wrote to me and said that he would like certain books out of the History Library, which he had donated. Perhaps I could find them and send them to him? And secondly, he would send a lot of his books to the History Library. I had to look after all of this. I enjoyed it, although it was a bit of a job. At the end of it he gave me one of the books he'd illustrated, for he was a graphic artist as well.

Another time one of the Professors gave me something to do, it was at Christmas of my final year, when I was trying to get ready for Mod. Curtis asked me would I go through all the history journals of the last year, which were to be found in the National Library. He gave me a list of these journals, and I was to look through them all and see what kind of reviews he got with his latest publication. Goodness! That took me the best part of a week. Today, they wouldn't ask such a thing of a student, they wouldn't get away with it.

I used to go and read in the Reading Room, which was entered through the Memorial building, erected just before I came to Trinity, in memory of Trinity people who had fallen in the First War. It had been opened only in 1937. It was always very moving to go into the Hall and see the 454 names of those killed, sometimes two and three brothers from the same family. The Oxford Colleges and the Cambridge Colleges have the same. It is absolutely devastating to look as you go in; the flower of our countries, destroyed.

There was the Elizabethan Society and the History Society. Of course, we had nothing to do with the men's societies, the Phil or the Hist. No women were in those. I had to wait for my daughter's time for that. Otherwise I tended to go back to Fitzwilliam Street, or to Trinity Hall. Quite often I would go out to see some of my relations. My Uncle Charlie, who was Diocesan Architect for Dublin and Meath, would let me know if he was going down to the country to inspect a Rectory or a Church, and he would take me with him.

Uncle Cyril was doctor to the Gaiety, the official doctor to travelling companies of theatrical people who came in from England. For that they gave him two spare tickets for the dress circle every Monday night, and I accompanied him to many plays, which I had never had a chance to see before. That was very stimulating. Meanwhile, I had a pretty steady boyfriend for a while, but I didn't have time to become involved in a serious relationship.

I was working for Mod, and I worked very hard. In fact, I got a bit dizzy, I couldn't see. I went to see an oculist, and she said, 'You're overstraining your eyes. Your eyes will be all right, but don't read for a week.' Luckily, my friend Betty Harman, who lived down in the country in Oldcastle, had said to me if I ever wanted to go down there in the summer, they'd be very glad to have me. So, I took her up on that, and I went down, and it was lovely. They had tennis parties nearly every day at that time of the year. There was a great crowd of tennis-playing people, and I was getting on with my tennis, better than I'd been before. I really enjoyed myself. For a week I was given good country food. Betty had one sister, Rose. We all had such a good time, and that was my break that year. When I got back to settle into working for Mod again, I could read. My eyesight had been rested.

It was a great surprise to me to do so well in Mod. although I had worked so hard. When it was over, Fanny Micks, whom I'd known as a student, and who was now the wife of Dr Robbie Micks, rang me up. She said, 'Would you like to come for a drive?' This was the day after Mod. was over, and it was so very kind of her. I said, 'Yes, indeed I would, very much.' So she took me out in their car, and I just felt absolutely shattered. My head was spinning.

Almost immediately, Uncle Cyril and Aunt Maureen took me down to see Maureen's people in Cork. It was Whit weekend and we stayed for a time in Maureen's parents' house, near Cork. I began to relax.

Before term was fully over, Miss Cunningham had gone into Sir Patrick Dun's Hospital with some kind of ailment they hadn't been able to diagnose. Robbie Micks was the Chief Physician there, and he diagnosed her correctly. But the prognosis was hopeless, and Miss Cunningham died before the end of June that year, which was quite a shock for us all. She was to have retired in June, and to have lived up in Donegal with two sisters, near the place from where they had come. Her death really upset me. A sad ending to an extraordinary part of my life.

9

COURTSHIP AND MARRIAGE 1940–41

Strangely enough, Donald was appointed Fellow of Trinity and I was made a Scholar on the same day, in June, 1939. We were on the same list, although neither of us noticed the other. And strangely enough I had cut out of the newspaper a photograph of somebody I knew, at the Trinity Races. When I came to put the photograph in my scrapbook after I was married, there exactly on the other side was a photograph of Donald with Provost Thrift, just after Don had been elected Fellow. That was the beginning. I didn't keep it originally for his photograph, but I put it in my scrapbook that way, afterwards.

I had no idea who was going to be elected in Classics. That year, there were two pre-elections. At that time, they had given up having that rather fierce exam for Fellowship. Now, what a prospective Fellow had to do was to give two oral pre-elections in the Exam Hall, or in the Public Theatre, as it was sometimes called. All the History students were very interested in this process in 1939, because our Professor Phillips was retiring and his successor would be appointed as a result of the pre-election. The History school, which, at that time was quite a large contingent, about twenty-five of us, all turned up to hear the pre-election of Theo Moody. It went on for a long time, but we were interested. Moody chose one of Phillips' pet subjects in which to give his pre-election, and I thought that was very brave of him.

When Moody's presentation was over, Donald's turn came, and we weren't a bit interested in who was going to be Fellow in Classics. We all trooped out. Donald often said afterwards that when he went in to give his pre-election, there was the Board in full regalia, he was in white tie, it was twelve thirty in the morning, but what he saw was the bulk of students squeezing out through the door, of which I was one.

At this time, Professor Curtis called on Donald who was now living in College rooms. Curtis brought Monsignor Paddy Brown[4], who was President of University College Galway, and who became such a good friend of Provost McConnell, recommending that McConnell should approach the Department of Finance for a grant, which had never happened before. This evening, Curtis and Brown brought with them an old Orange Flute, for they felt it was the way to welcome Donald to Trinity. Donald was an Englishman, and they played their special flute to entertain him. That is a side of Curtis I didn't know.

The next time that I came across Donald was when he was Junior Proctor at Commencements, and I started to sign my name, as I had on all my papers, surname first. I began to make a 'W', when a rather deep voice said, 'I said Christian names first.' It was Donald.

After I had graduated from Trinity, and was wondering what on earth to do, I felt very unsettled because the war was on. Should I join one of the services, which didn't attract me very much? I decided to wait until the Mod. results came out in October, and by then I was already doing some research on the Famine, supervised by Theo Moody. I had a little continuing money from Schol, and Uncle Cyril and Aunt Maureen very kindly offered me lodging. They now lived up the street from their former place, in 44 Fitzwilliam Square.

But I was very restless. With the war just across the Irish Sea, and all my Canadian friends in it, I began to think I really must move on somewhere and give up the research. And also I began to think that I wasn't really a research person. I liked it a certain amount, I enjoyed what I was doing, but it was too isolating for me. I didn't know what to do, where to go. I couldn't possibly go back to Canada with the Atlantic full of U-Boats and I remember walking round Stephen's Green one evening. I walked round and round and round because I didn't feel I belonged anywhere, I didn't know where I was going, or what was going to happen.

Theo and Margaret Moody had a party to which they invited me, and there

---

4   More formally Monsignor Pádraig de Brún President 1945–1959

was Donald Wormell. I knew he was the new Fellow in Classics but I didn't know anything else about him. One day afterwards I got a letter on my desk in the National Library where I was working, doing research. It was from Donald. I couldn't read his writing, half of it escaped me and I asked my friend, Doris Wilson, who was also working in the library, if she'd come outside. We went out onto a little balcony you could get to from the reading room, and there she deciphered the letter for me. It was asking me to a dance, in the Metropole Ballroom. What excitement! I went, and the other two people in the taxi were Walter and Olive Freeman. I remember very vividly, I was collected in Fitzwilliam Square by a taxi with a big balloon on the top. That was the way, then. It was a gas balloon – gas to power the taxi. There was no petrol whatever. So we went down to the Metropole in this taxi. And we also had one coming back. And I didn't quite know what to make of it because Donald let me get out of the car and he didn't come to the door with me at my uncle's house, and I thought that was very strange.

However, I paid no attention and not long afterwards he asked me to tea in his rooms in College. Also there were recently married Tony Werner and his wife. She was a Welsh opera singer, and we listened to music, which was very pleasant. But they followed the score which I couldn't do, so I thought 'Goodness, how am I in this circle?' But I found it pleasant. And then I left and went home.

A little while later, the Classical Association, a very lively group at the time, run by students, had a little dance in the Country Shop. Donald asked me to go with him, and to have a meal in the Unicorn, which was the restaurant very close by. And there were Bedell and Dorothy Stanford, with whom we had a nice evening. We went on to the dance, and then Donald this time did see me home, but he walked me all around Pembroke Park, first. I got home about two o'clock and the dance, which had started at eight, must have finished by twelve midnight. So we did a lot of walking.

Donald asked me to tea again, and then this time there were no Werners, no music lessons, and he more or less proposed to me, there and then, and I more or less accepted. When people ask 'How long did you court?' I say 'A matter of weeks,' but I also add 'It's not the best way.' We had thoughts of marrying in August, and this was in May, but as the days went on I began to find it all too much. I got quite sick, I was nervous. Eventually we decided that we would put it off. We would have to marry in the holidays; there was no hope of getting away during the term. So we put the wedding off until

12th December 1941, which was a long time to have to wait. It gave me time to catch my breath and for us to find a house. Some of the landladies asked, 'Hey! Are you two married?' We couldn't find a house.

There was some opposition from my family to the marriage, especially by Uncle Cyril, and it spoiled our engagement, because things were not easy. I still didn't know where I was going or what I wanted to do. My Aunt Vera Murphy kept settling me down. 'If you don't marry that man,' she said to me, 'I'm the one that's going to be upset. Do you love him?' 'I do, I do,' I replied. 'If so, you couldn't possibly not marry him!' she declared. Don and I went out to the Phoenix Park. We talked about everything. What an awkward conversation; I could hardly find a way to start it. But Donald was marvellous.

We went off on our bicycles. We were great cyclists and spent our engagement time cycling all over the place. One time we took sandwiches and had our lunch out in Shankill and that was wonderful.

Going away to Portsalon, in Donegal, with Herbert and Nan Parke, and their young daughter, Anstice, being with people who acted normally towards us and especially towards Donald, was very good. Don and I went cycling way up Knockalla Mountain, between Port Salon and Rathmullen. We climbed to the top, and there we settled it. A picnic, a quiet time, being left alone, that's what we needed. It was time I made my own life and followed my heart.

It was early September when we came back to Dublin from Donegal, and that's when I moved out of Uncle Cyril's place, staying in a flat on Elgin Road until the night before my wedding. I did sleep at 44 Fitzwilliam Square that night, but I was not happy about being there. I was completely on my own. The reception the next day was to be held at No. 44, and Uncle and Aunt were busy with the staff down in the kitchen, getting ready for the party. I didn't see anyone at all. I just stayed alone in my bedroom all evening.

My wedding dress had been made by Miss Anna, a dressmaker of some repute. As the wedding was in December, I chose a warm, brocade material. The bridesmaids wore a deep shade of pink, called Old Rose. Nan Parke helped me pick out the flowers for the bouquets. We decided on a shower-like, long arrangement that went down to the floor, and we used only white flowers. There was concern that if we used coloured flowers, such as pink to match the bridesmaids dresses, these would come out as black blobs in the black and white photographs.

Aunt Olive came on the day, and she helped me dress. And then my two bridesmaids, Betty Harman and Doris Wilson came in. They had nowhere else to change, and I insisted that they should be able to dress in the house. It was a cold house, and I was terrified Nan Parke, who was there dressing Anstice, our youngest bridesmaid, would get a cold. I remember getting very cross, saying that there would have to be more heat in the bedroom. Nothing was as it would have been if I had been in my own home. My mother would have given the kind of welcoming and wedding that you would expect from a normal household. So it was just very unfortunate. And another aunt of mine by marriage said that when I came up the aisle in the church on Uncle Cyril's arm, she said to herself, just from looking at my uncle's expression, 'I wonder what's wrong now in that family.' Uncle Cyril still didn't want me to marry Donald. But by that time I really didn't care. Uncle Cyril didn't come into the vestry when we were signing the vestry book. Uncle Charlie had always liked Donald, and his youngest son, Edward Murphy, was our pageboy.

I had a godmother, Edith Cooper, who had lived in Canada but had come back to Ireland. She was at our wedding, and I decided she was the person I would like most to have my flowers. She was the only one present who had also been at my parent's wedding in Calgary, and we asked her to sign the register.

Cyril and Maureen left the church as soon as possible, going off early in Uncle Cyril's car, for which he had petrol, being a doctor. One of my other uncles had petrol, too, but unfortunately he got drunk before the service. He had just got a movie camera and used to film family events, but it all came out just a jumble. Fortunately for everyone, there were some taxis outside the church.

I felt glowing at that stage. Having got through all of this immense upheaval, now everything was happily settled. Some pictures were taken. The one set of photographs I did get were from a man called Jack Coady. Ours was one of his first weddings. He hadn't been asked to come, he just arrived. He took a photograph inside the church, which Archdeacon Sullivan did not favour, but anyway Jack did it, and it is nice to have the picture. *The Irish Times* took one which they published. Then a sudden thunderstorm started, and many people were caught in it. For example, when the Moodys came in for the reception, they looked like two drowned rats.

We had little snacks at the reception, and I bought the wine and the champagne. I knew that my parents would have done this. I managed out of the little bit I had saved from teaching the Bradbury children. Ned Furlong, a future Trinity Professor of Moral Philosophy, was Donald's best man and he had interviewed a driver with a horse and trap. We went away in his horse and trap. I wore a going-away gown, specially designed, a black dress with gold all around. I was fortunate it was still early years in the War, and I could have such a lovely dress. We left the house and we went to Elgin Road to get rid of the confetti. When Doris, who had been a bridesmaid, came back afterwards to the flat, she said she'd never seen such a mess[5]. Confetti was all over the sitting room. Then the horse and trap took us to Kingsbridge Station, and we caught a train down to Naas, where another horse and trap met us, and took us to the hotel. The next day we took a train down to Cork and Kerry, where we spent our honeymoon.

---

[5] When Daphne was recording her memoirs and Anstice heard this description of scattered confetti, Anstice finally made a confession. She said, 'Pageboy Edward Murphy and I stuffed all the confetti we could find at the wedding reception into Donald's closed umbrella, in the hope that he would get showered on. He must have opened his umbrella inside the flat!'

10

CAMBRIDGE & BLETCHLEY PARK
1941–44

To be married in St Ann's Church I had to do residence in the parish. I had not been living in that part of Dublin, so I stayed in Buswell's Hotel for about ten days. On the Sunday morning Don came in for breakfast. There was always a paper waiting on the breakfast table, and that day the headlines reported that Pearl Harbour had been attacked. This was followed fairly quickly by the sinking of the two large battleships that the British had positioned to protect their interests in the East. Singapore and Malaysia are in the centre of that area, where there is a half circle of islands going outwards. One battleship was guarding one entrance to the semicircle, and another battleship was situated near the Philippines, guarding the other entrance. The Japanese went ahead after Pearl Harbour, and sank both those battleships. A battleship is a very serious loss. Those events were mixed up with our wedding.

In January, 1942, when we were home from our honeymoon, and established in 25 Palmerston Road, Singapore fell. The interest in Ireland was very great because so many Trinity people were out in Colonial Offices. Several dozens of graduates were in Singapore and in the Philippines, and some more were on the battleships. A family we knew had a son who was on one of the battleships. He was rescued and was put on a Japanese ship to be taken, as a prisoner of war, to Japan. The British torpedoed the Japanese ship and all the prisoners on board were drowned. What a tragedy! There is a plaque in the Cathedral in Singapore, listing the lost prisoners' names, which I sought out and found when I was visiting there, many years later.

Don could not get to England until we had been married about three months. Prior to that, there was no question of our going over. We were both unhappy about the extended neutrality in Ireland, when so many awful things were happening at the hands of the Germans and the Japanese. It was a worrying and difficult time. We were very unsettled, and Don particularly, being an Englishman, was restless. He wanted to participate, but he was somewhat hesitant. Of course, he could have signed up as a private, and crossed the Irish Sea at once. But he felt that, as an academic in his mid-thirties, he could likely contribute more in another area.

I had a very good friend who worked in the British permit office in Dublin. She always had the latest information about the situation, and she visited us one day, saying, 'There's going to be a lifting of the ban on British people going back to England, either to work, or to see their relatives.' We waited, and, sure enough, it came up. That meant that Don could go. We went through all the rigmarole of applying, and eventually, at Easter, the permits to travel arrived. Don had written to the Home Office enquiring how he could help as he spoke German, and they replied, asking him to come in to see them. An interview was arranged in London, when he was told, 'You would be very much needed at Bletchley.' We returned to Dublin, as we had to terminate our lease for our maisonette, although we had spent a lot of money setting it up. We packed up all our stuff, putting much of it into storage, where the moths got in; a great cloud of moths. The chairs were repaired afterwards, but for three and a half years those tweed moths had a lovely time.

We left for England together, and travelled to Cambridge, where I was to stay with Don's parents. I was pregnant, and I had to find somewhere to have the baby. In Ireland at that time, a gynaecologist would have been at the delivery. My doctor had sent a note from Dublin to the specialist in Cambridge, but the specialist did not want to have anything to do with me. So I went to a local doctor whose consulting room was close to where Don's parents lived. I was due in six months, but it was virtually impossible to arrange for a place in a Nursing Home, as there was an eight-month booking wait. All the young women, whose husbands had been conscripted and shipped off, were pregnant and they had booked out the Nursing Homes. We had to settle for what was not considered a very good Home, but at least it was close to Don's parents' house. They were approaching their seventies, and were very excited, as they had no grandchildren. Every able-bodied young person had to do something for the war effort, whereas if one was pregnant, it was acceptable to stay at home. Being pregnant was preferable to being trained and trying to settle into a job. One was given special consideration, and good food rations.

Don went to Bletchley, and was billeted with Mrs Baird, a local woman in a place called Bradwell. Her son had been taken prisoner at Dunkirk, and she worried about him. She had the radio on all the time, because she thought at the end of one of the broadcasts they would say, 'The War is over.' This was 1942. Like so many English people, she did hear occasionally that her son was alive, but she was particularly concerned that he had not answered her one question. Every time she wrote, she would ask him, 'Are your top false teeth safe?' 'They were very good,' she would tell Don, 'Ever so like a little fan, and I would hate to think that he has lost them.'

Mr Baird, the landlord, took Don on a tour of the small house, upstairs and downstairs, and then out to the garden. He said, 'The lavatory is out there, should you ever need it.' The next morning, Don found there was only one wash basin in the house, and that was the kitchen sink, and that was where he washed and shaved. Clothes that had been recently washed were hanging up above the sink, and coming down on his head, while the landlady sat in a chair and questioned him about his life, his work and his wife. Don said it was a startling change from what he had known the week before, having just come from a roomy, comfortable flat in Dublin.

Meanwhile, I was rather lonely in Cambridge. I had come from a very close student circle back in Dublin, students from my College days. In Cambridge I knew no-one, except Don's parents whom I had scarcely met, and Don's brother and his wife, both of whom were very busy with war work. However, after about six weeks, Don managed to find a place for us in New Bradwell, in a roomier house, where we were given a bedroom and sitting room to ourselves. I was very glad to be able to get to New Bradwell, primitive as it was. Our new landlady, Mrs Breeden, was a particularly amenable woman. We all shared a little kitchen. I was new to cooking, new to housekeeping, and it was a bit trying. The kitchen was a passageway and it made for a lot of difficult situations. However, I learned to keep out of the kitchen while the landlady was in the house. I would let her get off to work in the morning and then I would go into the kitchen. We also shared the house with a large, prize-winning chow dog, which took up a good deal of room.

It was a pleasant, quiet time for me. I went out walking and I prepared meals for Don. He was on shifts at the time, but we saw quite a lot of each other. A special bus collected Don, and took him the nine miles to Bletchley. Some days he didn't have to go to work until about four. The summer was coming on, and we would go for picnics, and I did a lot of reading. We had shipped some things from Dublin, mostly food, such as coffee, because you couldn't get these items in England. I had prepared hot-buttered eggs in Dublin. This was a preservation technique that my mother had taught me, rolling fresh eggs in their shells in hot butter, which sealed the shells and prevented the eggs inside from going bad. Any Irish country person always hot-buttered their eggs. It was mother's way. That's the way mine were, and they had always stayed fresh. When the Customs in Holyhead saw the eggs, they told us, 'Those won't keep.' So they confiscated them – and ate them all.

The first shift for Don went from eight to four. If he had the second shift, from four to twelve midnight, by the time he got in I would have gone to bed. I used to leave him sandwiches. I remember it was a bad place for spiders as it was a very wet summer, that summer of '42. One night Don came in, there was the plate of sandwiches on the table and a huge spider with one foot on them, guarding them as it were. Luckily, neither Don nor I had a spider phobia.

At this time I began to lose my hair. It was caused by pregnancy, and it was a sign of strain. I happened to be subject to it. I did go to some doctors at the time, but they all said, 'Wait until the baby has been born.' I remember going over to Bradwell to visit Mrs Baird, and she had a good look at my hair, and she said, 'You know, you'd have been much better to lose your teeth.' Maybe I could have had a nice little fan plate, then, too!

One night I fell down the stairs, tripping over the dog. I lay at the bottom of the stairs, worried stiff. Maybe I'd have a miscarriage? Or, even worse, maybe I'd damaged the baby? The landlady was very sympathetic, picked me up, gave me a cup of tea, and then took me up to bed. Both the baby and I had escaped harm. Don said he had had an awful premonition that night when he was being driven home in the bus, that something had happened to me.

There was a lovely bluebell wood nearby. I used to go out walking and I would take the little *Observer Book of Flowers* because the wildflowers of the British Isles were strange to me, since I had been brought up in the Prairies in Canada. I learned much about flowers in those few months. It was a peaceful time.

Don did not really like the work at Bletchley. It was supposed to be secret, and certainly Don never revealed much to me. Even in his last years, he was very critical of people who discussed their activities at Bletchley, though others apparently thought it acceptable. He always said he had taken an oath about secrecy, and he felt that he should honour it.

Don was breaking codes. The Channel ports, all along the North Sea, and down towards the Bay of Biscay, were in German hands, and the Germans would signal to each other by radio. They changed their code every day, and the great thing was to try to break this code as quickly as possible. The words of the broadcast would be on Don's desk when he arrived, and he had to work out the code being used that day. Speed was imperative as lives would be at stake. The code breakers worked from the idea that 'e' is the most common letter. Of course, it was in German; that was why Don was there at all. Among all the crude remarks and the silly, flippant jokes that were transmitted, there would be one message that had military significance. To sort the messages the code breakers would go through all the dross hoping to find the little bits of gold. Don was in his mid-thirties at this time, and he said that the young people, just coming out of College, or even occasionally just out of school, had minds that were the quickest and the best at code cracking. There were some very interesting people working with him, about eight altogether.

Frequently, Don would come in from work, and in our small room he would pace around and around. He was trying to settle himself down after the day's work because it would have been hectic, and he would have been under great pressure to break the code quickly.

He did tell me that his shift was working the day of the 'Dambusters'. The code was cracked early enough to be of help to the bomber plane crews. The Germans were fooled for a time, long enough for the mission to succeed. But the Germans eventually realised what was happening, and they came on with great force. The total casualty numbers for the British were high on that raid. Now it is discussed whether it was worth the price paid, as so many ace pilots were lost that night. It had been a beautiful piece of practical physics, developing bombs that could bounce along the water when dropped at specific angles. It had been thought that the effect of breaking the dam and drowning that part of Germany along the Rhine, would have had more disastrous results, but, of course, the Germans coped.

The time of greatest tension for the code-breakers was around D-Day, as all the German-held ports were being threatened. Bletchley put people not on two, but on three consecutive shifts. Don was working around the clock at that time. He rarely saw any daylight. The buildings at Bletchley had bombproof windows, which meant they were also sun-proof.

In December, with baby's due date towards the end of the month, and with Christmas approaching, Don was given a few days off and we set off for Cambridge. The train from Bletchley to Cambridge was delayed that night, and we arrived very late. The buses had stopped running, most cars had been commandeered, and there were no taxis to take people like us across the town to Don's parents' home. It must have been a two or three mile walk, it was cold, and we had luggage to carry. I was very exhausted when we got in.

It was thought that the baby might be due on Christmas Day, but Richard was phenomenally late. After Christmas, Don had to return to Bletchley, but he did get time off for a couple of days together. One day, each week, he would come up to Cambridge in the evening, he would have a free day, and then he would return late the next day. It so happened that he was in Cambridge when Richard was born, which was very satisfactory.

My diary from that time best describes events:

Christmas Eve, 1942

Listened to Carol Service from King's. We could hear planes overhead, flying above the service. Very sweet voices. Nine Lessons. Walked in the evening, lovely orange moon rising. Spotted Jupiter, Orion's Belt, and Saturn. Russians are doing excellently.

December 28th, 1942

I studied Eliot. Eliot believes that poetry deals only with aesthetic values, and has no relation with philosophy, morals, metaphysics. Eliot is a leader for his generation because he has been on his way somewhere. 'Ash Wednesday' has more imagery than former poems. But phrasing, cadences are brooding. I thought all good.

December 31st, 1942

Russians claim the Germans 'are doing a Rommel' south of Stalingrad. 'Junior' refuses to catch the last bus of 1942, not wanting to be born this year.

January 1st, 1943

Pram is ready in Ward's. It looks spiffy, like a Rolls Royce production. War prams have little spring, and are limited as to metal. Consequently, they frequently have wooden frames. Went to see Dr Walker, told him I was right about Junior not coming until New Year. He said to try 2 oz. Castor Oil and a hot bath in the morning. I have made my last will and testament. Very restless. Reading Arthur Gray's *History of Cambridge*.

January 3rd, 1943

Slept badly because of apprehension over Junior, and excitement too. At 8:20 pm took my castor oil, and at 10:20 my hot bath. Slept till 12:30 today, feel perfectly fit!

January 8th, 1943

Don arrived last night. Junior may tonight! Went into Nursing Home about 5:00 p.m.

January 9th, 1943

Richard Oliver Wilson born at 11 a.m. Weighed 8 pounds. Don saw him before he was clothed. Came out of the anaesthetic to hear the nurse, who had just met Donald, exclaim, 'I always say Donalds have nice, big comfortable faces like his.' Never tasted anything so delicious as my cup of hot chocolate and two digestive biscuits, which they gave me for lunch.

January 9th to January 20th, 1943

In Milton Road Nursing Home. Progress maintained. On iron pills as Doctor said I was rather pallid.' We're looking for a gas-proof container for Richard.

January 22nd, 1943

Russia marches on. I have a gnawing loneliness inside me these days; it won't be so bad when I'm doing things again. Letter from Mum: Brian has now got to the sniffy stage – oh! dear! – I am nothing because of our choice of 'Richard' as a name.

Although Don was back working, I stayed on in Cambridge with Richard, who was a very fractious baby. He wouldn't settle down at all, and I discovered the real reason was that I was breast feeding him, and I didn't have enough milk. The doctor came in one day when Richard was screaming in the middle of the afternoon, and the doctor said, 'That baby needs a bottle pushed into his mouth.' So he gave me a recipe for a formula to make up bottles, and I supplemented the baby's diet for a while. Later on, when Richard was about two and a half months old, I was able to breastfeed him without supplements.

At that stage we took Richard back to New Bradwell, to the Breeden house. The rooms were very small, and while I was bathing Richard in the sitting room, Don would have to go upstairs, or go for a walk, because there wasn't room for him as well as the table, the chairs, the baby's bath and the various bits and pieces required for a baby. So Don would clear out, and return when the bathing was over. Of course, we had to keep the chow dog out of our part of the house, all the time.

There was a wonderful busybody who lived across the road. Her name was Mrs Earp, and she took it upon herself to look after me. She thought it was disgraceful having a dog in a house where there was a baby. She would bring in some disinfectant, and she would spray it all around the hall, throwing it up in the air. It was ridiculous. If I was changing Richard, she would cast her eyes up to the ceiling, and say, 'Oh yes, I knew a little Richard once. But he died at seven months. What a long baby yours is! Yes, the other little Richard was three feet, nine inches in his coffin.' It became a joke. Don would come home in the evening, and ask, 'What did Mrs Earp say to you today?'

I had no friends there. I felt somewhat lonely. As soon as I was able to take Richard out in the pram, I was a little better, as I could go for walks. But there was nobody to talk to, except for a couple of women who lived across the street. I sometimes fell into step with them, pram pushing. They would talk a lot about the Bletchley people, that there was a spy among them that had been caught. One declared, 'You'd never think she was a spy, because she talked ever so well off.' One time, Richard's pram ran away and was saved from rolling onto the road by an old gent.

Unfortunately, the man in charge of Don's section in Bletchley, Hudson, was very unpleasant. Don said his whole approach was very devious. Later on, a friend gave our baby a homemade toy. Everything was so very scarce, even to look for material to make a child's soft toy was a hopeless task. So our friend cut up a fur coat and made a long doll, of which our baby grew very fond. It was made using comfortable, dark brown fur, and it had a little red tongue and a pair of beady eyes. Don took one look at the doll, and said, 'Oh, Hudson, that's its name!' So we never called it anything but Hudson. We very rarely had any kind of recreation, but one night we did go out to a pub. The pub was almost 'a pub with no beer', and a very inferior kind of beer was served. Sitting in there was Hudson! I was introduced, and I took one look at him and I knew what Don had meant when he had said the toy with the turned up nose and the beady eyes should be called Hudson.

March 10th–12th, 1943

Military manoeuvres – jeeps, armoured cars, lorries, staff cars, motor cycles, infantry, all passing day and night, many of them Canadians. Tanks came past in their dozens, among them a Calgary Corps. Gave tea and bread and jam to crew of a tank called 'Bucko.' Locals fed all who stopped. We found a cardboard container that had held a soldier's meal, measuring about six-by-four-by-one inches, and on which was printed DINNER. Planes overhead day and night. Don in the Home Guard wearing blue overalls and gum boots. Hopping over hedges and squirming under fences. Came across some taking it easy in a ditch. They called out 'Ride 'Em, Cowboy' and 'Come over and give us a lesson.' The Bucks County Council should send Ottawa a bill for damage to the woods. Caterpillars have dug up the edges; oil cans and bully beef tins fill the ditches; poultry is missing; it is even reported that they took six cows and a five-barred gate. Can this be the prelude to the Second Front? And did they choose Bucks for its similarity to some parts of France? Saw some children gathering primroses.

April 20th, 1943

Mein Führer's birthday. Celebrated it with a spring-beating of the carpet.

Nancy Larmour turned up around that time, and visited frequently. She had been two years junior to me in Trinity, but I hadn't known her very well then. She was feeling miserable because her fiancé was lost in the wilds of Burma and she didn't know his whereabouts. He had been trained as a civil servant for two years, and he had been sent into Burma on a plane, just as the Japanese were moving up the country. The Allies stationed there looked at him in amazement. Sending him in had been a big blunder. He appeared in his proper western clothes, carrying an umbrella, and wearing a hard hat! So they handed him a pair of shorts and said, 'Start walking.' Off he went, and eventually he walked out of the wilds of Burma. He then became attached to one of the regiments, but Nancy didn't hear news of him for two and a half years. It was difficult for her, and she was glad to visit us. She was working at Bletchley and staying nearby in a crowded hostel. Some evenings she and I would have the house to ourselves, Richard would be sleeping and we would both flop about and talk for hours. Nancy celebrated Richard's first birthday with us at the Bedford Arms, where we ate sticky buns and sandwiches, as Richard repeatedly shouted out 'Yum! Yum!'

Eventually, we arranged for someone to come in and clean up the kitchen, so that Mrs Breeden wouldn't be upset at seeing a mess on getting home from work. I remember Mrs Breeden saying that her husband was abroad somewhere in the army. 'I have a son of fourteen now. I can be expecting old buck out of him at any moment.' When I hear mothers talking about their teenagers today, I think of that comment.

After Richard was born we were given three rations. As Richard didn't need his, I could use the extra to occasionally go to the butcher. The women of that small community would be buying meat. They didn't like their husbands to see curlers in their hair. The wives would have waited until their husbands had left for work at about half past seven and then they would have put in their curlers. They would go out shopping with their curlers in. There would be such irrelevant conversations! I remember the butcher saying to one of them, 'You know, there was a civil servant in here the other day, and he told me he liked raw onions. Did you ever hear of a civil servant who liked 'roar' onions?' We had no phone, but we did get letters from overseas, and occasionally we received them from Ireland. We could reply giving local news, but we were not permitted to mention Don's work.

Finally, we heard of available space in a bigger house in a nicer district. So I borrowed a bike, and while Don looked after Richard, I rode over to Aspley Guise to investigate. The landlady seemed welcoming, and it was a beautiful house with large grounds. I returned to find that Richard had behaved himself, and that Don had washed up, swept up, made the bed, set the table and prepared a meal.

We decided to move. We now had two good rooms, the use of a big kitchen, and the garden was lovely. When we went down to the village there were better shops. Fish was available there, which was very good for Richard, as he was getting on to solids. But I did have my trouble with Mrs Weller, the landlady. She was a handful. There was already a WAAF billeted there. She told me, 'Don't be surprised if I'm not very friendly when Mrs Weller is about, because she gets very jealous. She reacts if I talk to other people, so I have to be careful.' A family called Fry also moved in, because Mrs Weller had said she would give up her bedroom, and sleep instead in the sitting room. Mrs Weller did have generous impulses, but when it came to coping, she was very house-proud, and she couldn't bear all of us using her kitchen. We weren't supposed to cook when Mrs Weller was there, so it was very awkward. Frequently, she would be upset because the Frys were too slow with their cooking, because the kitchen door wasn't being kept shut, because we were all on different shifts at work and were constantly in her way. Food was scarce. We each had separate rations, and we had to be careful not to take anyone else's rations.

Mrs Weller would say the most extraordinary things. I once asked her, 'Do you have a jelly mould I could borrow?' I knew the jelly would be lacking in taste, but a mould would make it at least appear appetising. 'I have twenty-nine,' she replied. Another time she said, 'If my mother-in-law liked the look of some kind of material she was going to have made up for a dress, she'd just go out and buy the whole bolt.'

Mr Weller was pleasant, but he was a dentist with the troops and he was away most of the time. They called their house Dingley Dell, after *The Pickwick Papers*, and they filled the house with things. One day Mrs Weller said, 'This is going to be my brass day!' So she collected all the brass from all over the house, including a Buddha that sat in the dining room where we had our meals. She hadn't liked the Buddha when she was first married, and she had put it out of sight in the garage. She had had very bad luck for the next nine months, so she brought it back into the house again. She respected it very much, and was diligent about cleaning it.

They had designed the house, and every room represented a different century. The dining room had a stone floor, but what century that was I don't know! One time, when Don was eating a meal, he looked down and noticed there was a carving in the flagstone. It said, 'In memory of ...' When the Wellers had gone to the stone masons to get flag stones for the floor, the stone mason had said, 'You can't have that one.' 'Oh,' Mrs Weller said, 'Yes, I'll have it.' 'Well,' he said, 'You could put it upside-down, of course.' 'I wouldn't put it upside-down,' she said, 'It is much more interesting this way up.'

On the floor of the dining room were two hippopotamus feet, loose, that a friend had brought them from India. Richard loved those feet. He would happily go out the front door, pick up a stone, and come back, crawling across the flag floor, and put the stone in a hippopotamus foot. He repeated this until eventually he had many stones in each foot. On the wall hung a substantial bow with an arrow, and above the fireplace a bracket supported a loaded gun. We felt if a bomb came nearby, the whole lot would come showering down on us, arrows, guns, brass, all sorts of things.

Planes flew above us all the time. We could see glider planes, with blue and white stripes, and also Lightnings, dashing out in fours. Then the pilotless planes, the buzz bombs began. They were called 'queen bees' by the British and 'dynamite meteors' by the Germans. A buzz bomb made a unique noise. Suddenly it would go silent and we knew that in two minutes it would explode somewhere. It was nerve-racking. We would hear them buzzing right over us, on their way to London, as the Germans were trying to demolish the capital city. Many nights we carried Richard in his cot out of the bedroom into the landing, as that was less likely to collapse. Eventually the bombs would stop, and we would lift Richard and the cot back into the bedroom. We had such dreadful thoughts, hoping that the bombs wouldn't stop above us, that they wouldn't fall on us, that they would fall on someone else. None landed especially near to us, but their sounds were distressingly close.

A lot of damage was done in London, and people were told to get out of the city, if at all possible. Aunt Jane, my father's sister, came to stay near us. She had been living in a flat, in London, where she was a nurse. So we found her a bed in a nearby house, with a nice old lady called Mrs Oldfield, where she could sleep. There was a fellow called Oldfield back in Alberta whom I had known, and this Mrs Oldfield was his aunt. Aunt Jane had to spend the days with me, and she became yet another person in the kitchen. She didn't understand the business of separate food and organisation.

Mrs Weller had a cat which she and her husband had rescued when living in Southampton. She had brought it back on condition that it lived outside, that it caught its own food, that she didn't have to feed it. No one had any spare meat to give to a cat, and it had to take its chances outside, where there were wild rabbits. The cat didn't look at all starved. Mrs Weller would occasionally give it milk, and the cat would come into the kitchen looking for its milk. Aunt Jane was a great animal lover. She saw the cat come in one day, and she looked around for something to feed it. Mrs Weller had used rations from everyone to make a treat for us all, a treacle tart. It was on the counter, there were two or three pieces out of it, and Aunt Jane started to cut another piece to give to the cat. I can still remember Mrs Weller's outburst: 'Now, Miss Wallace, we can't have that kind of thing going on here...blah...blah.' I recall one conversation I had with Aunt Jane in that house. 'This is a lovely place,' she said. 'You know, when I'm in London, for my health I have to take two teaspoons of Epsom Salts and a teaspoon of olive oil everyday. Here, I only have to take one teaspoon of Epsom Salts, and no olive oil.' It was all a bit strange, like a pantomime.

Aunt Jane eventually returned to London, when the buzz bombs decreased. Germany was in a very bad way by this time. The morning of D-Day I went down the driveway to fetch the post, which was always left there in a mailbox. Don had gone off early to Bletchley, and the old gardener called out, 'They've started. They have landed near Boulogne and are bombarding *Deep*,' meaning Dieppe. Finally, the invasion had begun.

As the summer wore on, and the fighting was no longer in the European ports, Don didn't have as much work to do. The decoding and deciphering was not relevant anymore. The Allies were making a great push down to the Rhine that autumn and we hoped that all would be over by Christmas. Unfortunately the war continued; the Germans had an Ardennes offensive, and the disaster of Arnhem took place. The paratroopers were flown in, the Germans had wind of it early and were ready for the drop. So many of the paratroopers were killed, including the brother of a close friend in Dublin. The Padre with them was Alan Buchanan, who later on became Archbishop of Dublin. He could have escaped, but he decided to stay on and be a prisoner with the others. The fighting went on all through that winter. It was very sad, because we had thought the war would be over by that time, that it would all be finished.

Meanwhile Trinity had been losing staff. There was a shortage, and the Provost wrote to Donald saying that it would be very much appreciated if he would return. The people at Bletchley were sympathetic to Don being called back to Trinity, and released him late in October, 1944. He returned alone to Dublin, where he lived in his College rooms. Don was giving lectures, and trying to pick up again after the years away. He was told all aliens had to officially register, so he went to do so at the Garda Office, the police station near Trinity. He was asked, 'Why are you coming in here?' 'Well,' Don replied, 'I'm a British citizen.' 'And you're coming in here to register?' asked the policeman, who continued, 'Sure, we're all British citizens as far as I know.'

We had given up our apartment when we had left for England, and we had no place now in Dublin. We had decided that Richard and I should stay on with Mrs Weller, which we did for a month. Mrs Weller was in an awful fury before Don left. She had always been jealous that we could live together, while her own husband had to be away most of the time. Don went off to Dublin worried about what she might do to me. But the minute he left, she became all sweetness and light, and she helped me in many ways. She gave me a little Humpty Dumpty pepper pot, saying, 'In case I fight with you, you had better take this. It's a little gift from me to you.' I still have it and keep it on the table. It is a memento of a strange relationship.

Aunt Bessie, who was my mother's eldest brother's widow, had a house in Monkstown, in Dublin. When she heard Richard and I were left behind in England she wrote immediately, saying, 'Come and stay here.' So, I packed up everything, and we went by train to Holyhead to catch the ferry over the Irish Sea.

11

HOME AT MOUNT MERRION 1945–49

When I was bringing Richard back to Ireland, to live with Aunt Bessie, we had a very bad crossing on the ferry. I was so seasick I couldn't move, and I had to let Richard run around the boat. By this time he was two and a half, and, sure enough, he picked up chicken pox on that trip. Aunt Bessie was very kind to us, being especially good to Richard. She liked him and took him out a great deal. Every night he used to talk for two or three hours. Looking back on it now I know that he was hungry. He used to talk about his breakfast. I thought he was having too much food, or the wrong kind of food, but really he just needed a bit more, for he had a voracious appetite.

Don stayed on living in his rooms. He was able to come out for the odd night, and for the weekends, but it was easiest for him to continue to live in his College rooms. I began to look around for a place where we could live together.

Aunt Bessie was a widow, and her younger son, Willie, was living with her at the time. He, too, was practising as a doctor, although he later went to the south of England, and became an anaesthetist.

One morning I came down to breakfast, which was early so that Willie could get to his practice, and I picked up *The Irish Times* which was delivered in those days in good time for breakfast. I quickly turned to 'houses for rent' and saw a house listed in Mount Merrion, not far from where we were staying and a bit closer to Dublin. I knew the area, and I recognised the house. A telephone number was given. I said to Willie, 'I should ring.' 'Oh,' said Willie, 'If I were you, I'd ring at once.' Surprised, I said, 'At eight o'clock in the morning?' 'Yes,' he said. I rang up and I told them that we were interested. The rent was mentioned, and it was arranged that we would we go around in the evening and view it. We fixed it up before we went to bed that night, and afterwards I discovered that the phone belonged to the neighbour – they didn't have a phone in 37 Greygates. And they told me we had been the first to phone, and that was why we got the house. We were fortunate, as there weren't many houses available at that time.

It was a nice house, with four bedrooms, which was adequate. At last we had some space, and Donald could have a study. Val, my sister, came to live with us from Alberta, and she began her studies at Trinity, in Natural Sciences. Both Don and I felt strongly that we had each been given assistance at critical times, and that now it was our turn to do the same. It was wonderful for me to have a family member so close.

Mother came, too, for a visit, over the winter of 1946/7. It was a terrible winter, and no proper heat. Any heat from a small fire we had was used to dry the nappies, which hung wet from a wooden clothes horse which was set up like a fireguard, wrapped around the fireplace. Julia had been born earlier that year. I used to go to bed to get warm, because Mother had flu and was in bed all the time, Richard had flu and was in bed all the time, and Don had flu and was in bed all the time.

Then I got sick. At first, it was thought my nerves had become inflamed, while, in fact, I had minor polio; I had it in a mild form. The one good thing was that it inoculated me from having it badly another time. Mother got the doctor in one night. Don said Mother was in an awful state, and she wouldn't tell him what she was worried about. She thought I had polio, and I remember the doctor coming in and later on he called up two specialists, Dr Wilson and Dr David Mitchell. Dr Mitchell turned around to Dr Wilson and said, 'This is a very serious complaint.' I had severe pains in my left leg, but I got better gradually. However, my left side has never been quite right, and my mouth is slightly crooked. People say, well you don't notice it, and I say, well look at me in the mirror, and you will notice that I'm very slightly drooped. I remember going to town for the first time afterwards, and knowing that I must put my right foot out first, because the left foot wasn't strong enough. But I got over it.

We had a famous Sunday dinner party in Greygates. I had forgotten to order the joint, and I went around and got one offered by a friend, but she didn't have a proper one. It was one that you cook in water, but I said, 'Well, I'll do with that. Thank you very much.' The guests were a student who lived close by, Jack Duggan the Curate, and Val. I'm not sure if there was anyone else. Don tried to carve the joint, and it fell on the floor in the dining room. It was nothing to do with Don's carving; it just wasn't possible to carve the tough meat, that was the trouble.

I was dishing out the soup into bowls set out on the table, holding the blackened pot, and I said to Richard, 'Don't let them come in just yet.' So Richard raced in, swung open the living room door, and shouted, 'Everybody come in, fast!' Richard really was a little terror. It was the in-thing to mix the brown sugar in with the white sugar, so I thought I'd try that for this special occasion. Richard asked loudly, 'What's the brown sugar doing?' One of the guests at the table asked Richard what had happened that morning in Church. He replied, 'Well, Mr Duggan was all dressed up, and we heard the news.' Don said he thought that was quite a good summary of what had happened.

Silence fell at the table just as Val and I went out to the kitchen to get the dessert ready. The dessert had melted, and one of us said, in a loud voice, with silence in the dining room, 'What have you done, now?' I was very glad when that dinner party was over. I wonder if Duggan remembered it. He would have chuckled. He went on and became a Bishop.

In 1949, we bought a house as it was being built. It was on Sandyford Road, on the 44 bus route, and on the way to Enniskerry in Co. Wicklow. We named it 'Gatineau'. Robin had arrived, and we needed the space, outdoors as well as inside. It was the start of a new era for us.

c. 1918. Daphne, about 2 years old. Calgary.

*1924. First trip to Ireland, day after arrival.
On beach at Skerries, left to right front:
Dorothy, Daphne, Hugh. Back: Aunt Olive
Murphy, sister of Eva, Daphne's mother.*

Bowness, 1916. Wallace House, standing alone on the prairie.

6th September, 1928. A happy day at Fassett, Quebec. Left to right: front: Eva (née Murphy) Wallace, Brian, Val, Hugh; back: Daphne, Dorothy.

c. 1930. Daphne as a happy Ottawa teenager.   *Early 1932. Daphne's last winter in Ottawa.*

1935. Brownstown House. Daphne drives the horse and rake, helping 'to make the hay.'

Calgary, 1936. Wallace Family. Left to right: Front: James, Eva, Brian. Back: Daphne, Hugh, Dorothy, Val.

Members of the Dublin University Elizabethan Society Officers and Committee 1938–39, in front of No. 6. Back row: left to right: Daphne Wallace, Rose Gwynn, Ginete Waddell. Front Row: left to right: unidentified, Evelyn Nesbitt, Helen Tobias, Joyce McGilligan, Leslie Tyrrell (who provided photo).

Trinity Monday, Front Square, TCD, 1939. Daphne had just been awarded Scholarship. Left to right: Cyril Murphy (Daphne's Uncle), Vice-Provost Goligher, Vera Murphy (née Goligher and Daphne's Aunt), Daphne Wallace, Leo Murphy (Daphne's Uncle).

1941. Daphne taken by Donald, during their courtship.

1941. Don on one of the engaged couple's walks in the Wicklow hills. Daphne wanted a photo to send home to Calgary!

Portsalon Beach, August 1941. Left to right: Anstice Parke, Nan Parke, Daphne Wallace, Don Wormell.

December 12, 1941. Wedding Day. Photo taken at home of Cyril and Maureen Murphy, 44 Fitzwilliam Square, during the Wedding Reception. Photographer was Jack Coady. This was his first wedding assignment, his last being the wedding of Daphne and Don's daughter Julia, July 16, 1973.

Full wedding party of Daphne and Don, December 12, 1941. Left to right: back row: Professor Ned Furlong, best man; Don, Daphne, Doris Wilson and Betty Harman, bridesmaids. Front row: Edward Murphy (first cousin of Daphne) and Anstice Parke.

1947. Left to right: Daphne holding Julia, Richard, Donald. As displayed in the photographer's window in Grafton Street for several years, with the caption "And they lived happily ever after."

1952. Kitty (née Keating) O'Reilly with the Wormell children. Left to right: front: Robin; back: Julia, Kitty, Stephen, Richard.

Spring, 1953. About to enter the church for the wedding of Renée Fleury.

c. 1960. Gatineau, before any road building or granny flat development. Don's study window lower left, Nannie's bedroom window top, centre.

1968. Wormell Family. Left to right: back: Don, Daphne, Richard; front: Stephen, Robin, Julia.

1967. Elizabethan Society Garden Party, Trinity Week. Left to right: Daphne, Mary Boydell, Dr Brian Boydell.

1977. At Gatineau, in front of Don's flowers along the driveway. Just before attending a Trinity Week function.

1982. Daphne giving a talk on the RTE programme 'Outlook'.

July, 1983. Daphne at Lennon Family Reunion, Niagara-on-the-Lake, Ontario.

April, 1986. Patricia Hastings-Hardy and Daphne, fully robed, outside Canterbury Cathedral during the Ministry of Women Conference.

May, 1987. Wallace House on Golden Street, Ottawa.

Don after his retirement.

March, 1992. Daphne at the wedding of Susan, daughter of Betty Cole (née Harman), at Cloverhill, Co. Cavan.

1993. Approaching Daphne Island from the south, on the Athabasca River. The island is on the right-hand-side.

1993. Daphne on her island, Daphne Island, in the Athabasca River, north of Fort McMurray, Alberta.

September 1995. Daphne at home in her garden.

14 December, 1996, after conferring of Honorary Degree, in front of the Dining Hall, TCD. Left to right: Lyndall Luce, Dr John Luce Public Orator, Daphne, Dr Tom Mitchell, Provost.

16th November, 1997. Glencarrig Lodge, Delgany, home of Audrey Smith. A gathering of the first five female Lay Readers in the Diocese of Dublin and Glendalough. Left to right: Thea Boyle, Patricia Hastings-Hardy, Audrey Smith, Daphne, Joan Rufli.

19th November 2000. 25th Anniversary of Commissioning, Christ Church Cathedral, Dublin. Left to right: Canon Ginnie Kennerley, Daphne, Patricia Hastings-Hardy, Audrey Smith, Thea Boyle, Dean John Paterson.

2000. Bella Napier, 'Nannie'.

Summer, 2001. Daphne and Julia at Avoca Handweavers, Kilmacanogue, Co. Wicklow.

Outside Rathmichael Church. Left to right: Bishop Jack Duggan, Rector Billie Marshall, Archbishop Donald Caird, Archdeacon Donald Perrin, William Deverell, Lay Reader Daphne Wormell, Lay Reader Frank Luce.

Some members of the Women's Ministry Group Committee at a social evening held in TCD. Left to right: Margaret Gilbert Secretary, Jennifer Gill, Phyllis Faris, Desirée Wilson Treasurer, Daphne Wormell Chairperson.

PART TWO by Julia

12

DONALD

Originally, everyone assumed that when Daphne completed her undergraduate studies she would return home to Calgary. However, the Second World War had started, so travel was out of the question. She was stuck. But she had made some good friends in Dublin, and she liked being amongst so many Murphy family members. Having been highly successful in her studies, receiving a First Class degree, it was natural that she should spend this extra time on some post-graduate work. Theo Moody, Professor of Modern History, was happy to take her on as a postgraduate student. In Daphne's final year as a Modern History and Political Science student, in November 1939, Theo Moody had been in the first year of his lecturing in Trinity. Daphne's final essay of that year's work, held together with a sewing pin, helped her win a Gold Medal. It was titled 'The Responsibility of Louis XVI for the Fall of the Monarchy.' Prof. Moody's comments at the end of the essay were: 'An admirably reasoned and coherent essay, touching on most of the essential points and avoiding direct narrative wherever possible ... The style is inclined to be over-rhetorical, in my opinion, but so fluent, rigorous and individual that I hesitate to criticise it at all.'

However, she quickly discovered that spending hours alone was bringing on a form of depression. 'I was not suited to that type of endeavour, working on my own, being alone.' Her solution was to pull out of her studies. How fortunate that Theo and Margaret Moody used to give afternoon teas and that to one of these they invited both new TCD Fellow and Classicist, Donald Wormell, and graduate student, Daphne Wallace. In no time they were dating. It was difficult in those days to find places to be alone with a date in Dublin. Years later, when walking with Daphne along the canal, or driving by the locks, she would tell of the times she and Don had spent strolling there, arm in arm, seeking solitude. But mostly they took to the hills on their bicycles. There are many photographs taken with a Brownie camera of one or other of them sitting on a peak or with a mountain rising behind.

Not all of Daphne's relatives thought Don was suitable for Daphne. She was hearing comments from some of them. The worst seemed to be that Don looked unacceptably Jewish! This was not the best for someone in love, who was realising at the same time that her studies were not doing her any good. She wrote frantically to her mother in Calgary for advice. Eva wrote back that Donald sounded marvellous, and stated that anyone who knew their family history would be aware of the Jewish blood already flowing in Daphne's veins. This letter was intercepted, opened, read and destroyed. Daphne never saw it, only hearing of its contents from Eva years later.

Uncle Cyril had difficulty with Daphne getting married. I believe he was half in love with her. In her early twenties, Daphne had come to his house where he lived with his mother who was in her eighties, and no doubt Daphne brightened his life. He was an outgoing, charming man, well-known around Dublin and beyond, and Daphne acted as hostess for him at all his large dinner parties. She would have done the food shopping and would have organised the dinner. She accompanied him weekly to the theatre. She would dress appropriately, having been able to go clothes shopping with the pocket money Uncle Cyril slipped her way. He was intensely proud of her achievements at Trinity, and knew he had been an influence and support to her. At the time Daphne and Don were dating, Cyril was happily married, but Daphne had been the one to show him how a feminine presence could lighten a dreary Dublin evening. His possessiveness clouded his vision of Daphne's future. Other family members asked Daphne not to spread this around, and she followed instructions – until the walk with Donald through Phoenix Park, when she told him all about her troubling family pressures. Donald would have given her one of his big hugs, Daphne would have wept, he would have taken out his large white hankie to wipe away her tears, and he would have said, 'Everything will be all right. There's a good day coming.'

But Daphne's world seemed to be crashing around her. She left Dublin, and went into seclusion by the sea, in Co. Cork. She was in despair at not having heard from her mother, and she was learning that being alone was not good for her. She returned to Dublin, rested but still uncertain. She did agree to a seaside holiday in Donegal with Donald and the Parkes. Don and Herbert Parke were close colleagues in Trinity, they had great mutual respect for one another, they would co-author a book in the future, and each considered the other his best friend. Daphne and Nan Parke were becoming good friends. Anstice Parke, their daughter, recalls the time well, for she was a child and unable to understand how Daphne and Don could be so playful with her for a time on the beach, and then would want to wander off alone, leaving her with her parents, whose firm instructions were that she was not to follow. Nan talked common sense to Daphne, as she would for the rest of their lives. Nan was just what Daphne needed at that time. The decision to marry was made on Knockalla Mountain, and they all returned happily to Dublin. Daphne's friends rejoiced at the news. Doris Wilson rented a flat on Elgin Road, and removed Daphne from family influences.

At this time, Don held a small reception in his rooms in No. 40, in Trinity College. He wanted to celebrate his overwhelming happiness. His own family was far away over the Irish Sea, on the eastern side of England in Cambridge, and had hardly yet received the telegram bearing the news. So he invited his newly won family, all of Daphne's Dublin relatives, a great clan of Murphys. They were pleased to be visiting Trinity, many of them returning to where they had spent happy student years. Don had pushed back the furniture, and had brought in drinks and refreshments. But the Murphys were at odds with each other, not only over Daphne but also over many family issues that had risen over the years. They divided in that room into their various camps, and there was no communication between them. Don laughed about their hostile behaviour for years afterwards.

Wedding preparations were made. As Daphne describes in an earlier chapter, they were married in St Ann's Church, in Dawson Street, best man being Ned Furlong, a future Fellow of Trinity, and future Professor of Moral Philosophy. Betty Harman, Doris Wilson and young Anstice Parke were bridesmaids. The only relative in the wedding party was Edward Murphy, Uncle Charlie's son, who made a charming nine-year-old page boy. It had all happened so fast, as it was only months since the Moody tea party.

Don had grown up in Cambridge, the younger of two boys. His mother, Florence, had been a teacher, and had met her husband while teaching in Bristol. Don's father, Thomas, had become Principal of a Cambridge Elementary School, after accepting that as a Methodist he would not be appointed as Head of any Senior Secondary or Public School. Thomas had been given interviews all around England for such positions and many times he had been told, 'You are by far the best applicant for this post, but your religion prevents us from offering you the Principalship.' Thomas settled for the lower-level position, realising that at least in Cambridge his two boys might be recognised by the University on Entrance and be granted Scholarships. This is indeed how it turned out.

Don's brother Thomas Wilson, always known as 'Will', was five years older, an academic achiever who became Lecturer in Atmospheric Physics at Cambridge University. Will had studied as a post-graduate student under C.T.R. Wilson of the famous Cambridge Cavendish Laboratory, and was cited by Professor Wilson in the first sentence of his address on receiving the Nobel Prize for Physics as the one who had done the major research which had led to the granting of the award.

Don was the family baby. He was mischievous, his eyes twinkling in early photographs. Successful at school, his early reports say he could choose Sciences or Arts. Not wanting to follow his brother, he settled on the Classics.

At the Perse School, Don had the good fortune to be instructed by Dr W. H. D. Rouse, a teacher of genius who taught the boys by the Direct Method, speaking to them in Latin and in Greek as if these were living languages. Don and his classmates were drilled daily in correct pronunciation and enunciation, and the result was that Don could speak the languages fluently. When President Kennedy visited Ireland he was awarded a TCD honorary degree and it was the duty of the Public Orator, Professor Donald Wormell at the time, to deliver the oration in Latin. A film made of the occasion shows the seated U.S. President at first holding up the text to follow along, but on recognizing the quality of the reading, Kennedy puts down the paper on his lap and turns to listen more attentively. Dr Rouse's teaching also inspired his pupils to read and think broadly, and students were invited to his home on Sundays where he read to them many authors, such as Charles Dickens, for several hours.

Don's teachers were also disciplinarians. If he didn't have his homework done, an ink bottle or a blackboard eraser came hurtling towards his head.

But his report cards gave glowing comments, except for his handwriting, which even then was a scribble. Don's successes did not come without cost. As was the custom he was promoted into higher grades, finishing school when he was sixteen. He was as big as his classmates, but he was vulnerable in his immaturity. The bullying he was subjected to had long-lasting effects.

Don was a prop forward in rugby. He was known for his 'sharp shoulder blades' and he played for two years on the Perse School Senior Rugby Team, captaining the team in his final school year. He put much thought into how his team could achieve better results, and in the second half of his final season his efforts were rewarded with many more wins recorded by the senior team than before. Even after Don had gone on to University, his team continued to perform extremely well all through the following year, as the team members had learned to concentrate on the mental process in the preparation for a match. Early on, Don had come to realize the importance of concentrating on thinking about being successful as part of the process of achieving success. It was to hold him in good stead in years to come.

Don went on to study in Germany and at Yale. He was a Fellow at Cambridge for three years, a Junior Lecturer in Classics in Swansea for another three years and in 1939 he was elected to Fellowship in Classics at Trinity College, Dublin. He became Professor of Latin in 1942.

As a university student, Don would study all morning and all evening, and if weather permitted, he would play tennis every afternoon. On arriving at Trinity he played tennis in the Fellows' Garden where he was known for 'his long reach'.

When Daphne met him early in 1941 Don was shy, having grown up in a small, calm, and very quiet family. Regardless, he was always willing and fully aware of how he could support and care for his Daphne.

Daphne had come from a family with three girls. The three sisters all married men who were the opposite of their father, each husband being gentle and quiet. In contrast to Daphne's relationship with her father, Don's quiet, supportive ways gave Daphne the foundation on which to build. It may not have always been easy for him, but he was always there, positive, admiring and helpful. Before he married, Don had been more developed academically than he was emotionally, but after he married all that changed. He opened up and in his final years he became quite extroverted.

They fitted together well, complementing each other's personalities. Daphne loved social gatherings of every kind, and Don was swept along with her. When Daphne was involved with the struggle for the ordination of women in the Church of Ireland, Don would sit quietly in a front pew in a country church. Can you hear the whispers of the congregation behind him? 'He's a Professor up at Trinity, you know.' The stage would be set for what Daphne wanted to say. She would have driven there, as Don was a horrible driver. He would have done the navigating, as Daphne never did learn how to easily follow a map. As a team, they could go anywhere and cause an impact. They supported each other in all endeavours undertaken throughout their married life.

Keen on women's rights, Don spoke on a panel on this subject, in Dublin in the fifties. A Mrs Kettle responded to his ideas, and the newspaper headlines the following day declared, 'Professor makes Mrs Kettle boil.'

By the end of the 1960s Don was long overdue a sabbatical, and he chose to take it for a year in 1967–68. He later said it was 'one of the best years of my life for I was completely free to do research,' in contrast to his position in Trinity College, where his administrative duties as well as his teaching load left little time for research. He was offered a place at Princeton's Institute for Advanced Study to research in any subject in Classics relating to Ancient History. He had long been fascinated by 'Exile' and he decided to focus on this subject, choosing in particular three Latin authors: Cicero, Ovid and Seneca, all of whom were sent into exile.

The Institute for Advanced Study in Princeton is a few miles from the site of Princeton University, and it sits in a beautiful setting surrounded by trees and well-groomed lawns. An international community made up of academics largely from the United States, but also drawn from all over the world, comes to the Institute to study each year in three areas of expertise: physics, mathematics and history. The academic year runs from September through to June, and researchers and their families stay in apartments on site. Don and Daphne and Robin lived together happily. Daphne took courses in History, as well as one on Bernard Shaw, another on Theology and yet another on 'Communications and the Media'.

Many notable figures have spent time at the Institute, the most famous having been Albert Einstein. In 1967/68, a memorable figure was Carl Schorske, a Modern Central European historian, who won the Pulitzer Prize for General Non-Fiction in 1981. Don and Daphne also visited with Homer Armstrong Thompson, with whom Daphne felt a close affinity as Thompson had been born in Canada. Thompson was a leading classical archaeologist of the twentieth century, who specialized in Ancient Greece, and who had by this time almost completed the excavation of the Agora, the marketplace in Athens. Daphne and Don also spent time with Clarence Ver Steeg, a distinguished American historian, and with Jacob Talman, an Israeli historian.

Hermathena is a T. C. D. Review, founded in 1873 and published twice a year. The issue published in the Winter, 1987, No. CXLIII, was dedicated 'In honour of D. E. W. Wormell'. Tom Mitchell, who had succeeded Don as Professor of Latin and who had later become Provost, wrote as follows in the Preface:

> Donald Wormell held the Chair of Latin at Trinity from 1942 to 1978. It was a long tenure, during which classical studies continued to flourish at Trinity and to produce a succession of talented graduates who went on to win high distinction in academic careers in universities around the world. Professor Wormell deserves much of the credit for the remarkable record of the School at a time when changing conditions and perceptions were weakening the traditional role of Classics in western education. He was an inspiring teacher and a humanist in the best Ciceronian sense of the term, combining broad knowledge with a quiet eloquence and an unfailing civility. He also had a special gift for the Latin language, which showed itself in his skill in explication and interpretation of Latin literature, and which is vividly illustrated in the more than one hundred Latin Orations he produced as Public Orator from 1952 to 1970...
>
> Donald Wormell's career is also remarkable for his contribution as an administrator to the development of the College as a whole. For almost three decades he played a central role in guiding the College through an era of enormous change and expansion. He served as Senior Lecturer from 1952 to 1958 and again from 1964 to 1967. He was co-opted to Senior Fellowship in 1968, and went on to become Vice-Provost from 1973 to 1974. His long service in administrative posts makes all the more noteworthy his achievements as a teacher and scholar.

Some of Don's most distinguished students contributed articles for publication in this 1987 *Hermathena*. Ted Courtney wrote of how he and Don had collaborated in preparing the text for Ovid's *Fasti*: 'On this harmonious and, to me, instructive collaboration I look back with the greatest pleasure, as indeed I do on a relationship which started in 1950 with a teacher who had seen so many of his pupils themselves in turn become teachers of Latin in the universities of Ireland, Britain and North America.' In the notes for his contributing article, J. T. Killen wrote: '... Donald Wormell, whose lectures on Latin literature were one of the most enjoyable and stimulating features of the (excellent) Classical course at Trinity when I was a student there. (My wife, who was also taught by Donald Wormell, warmly endorses that verdict.)... it was Donald Wormell who first encouraged me to think of the possibilities of an academic career...'

As a parent Don was clear-headed and sensitive, with an intuitive understanding. He always knew if 'something was up' with anyone in the household, and he would pursue the trouble until it was resolved. With his kids he played cricket and French cricket. He took us fishing, he rowed us around in boats, and he played cards in the evenings. He spent many hours in the large garden digging, and feeding the worms to the local robins. The robin of the day would wait on the fence until Don flicked out a worm from the turned sods. Both parents encouraged us to read, and told us stories and myths at bedtime. A favourite vision we share of our Dad is watching him, oblivious to us, walking round and round on the landing or up and down in the hallway, lost in thought and muttering in conversation with himself.

Don spent many hours setting and marking exam papers in a number of subjects for the Entrance Exams for students from all over the world who were seeking entrance to the Royal College of Surgeons. His job was to decide not only if the applicant was up to the courses of study intellectually, but also if the applicant was likely to be a good doctor. For example, if an applicant was a bad speller in the English exam, would the student be otherwise capable of reaching a high level of achievement? Did the student show promise as a future doctor? It was a difficult task, and he did it for many years.

When Don died in 1990, a friend from the States phoned to say, simply, 'The great oak has fallen.' Over ten years later, Fred Appelbe gave the eulogy for Daphne. He said in part, 'She is ... in peace, – with her Donald, without whom, in truth, she was never truly at peace.' They loved each other deeply, they needed each other on a daily basis and each grew more and achieved more because of their relationship.

Daphne's sister, Val, whose life had been so affected by Wormell generosity, said she wept all night on hearing that Don had terminal cancer. Unable to sleep, she spent the dark hours at her dining room table at her home on Vancouver Island and wrote the following poem, which was read to Don before he died:

To Don

It is past midnight and I weep
Transported through space and time
Back to a mist-shrouded land
Of scholars and saints
And post war turbulence.

You had brought me over land and sea
To wider horizons
From slicing dogfish in unscheduled ice
To troubled International problem solving
When we knew how to Save the World.

Your money
Thrown to the wind
With exams missed.
Casting a jaundiced eye
On hurdling Little-go
You paid Grinds for me to conquer it
And never complained.

I remember your study
Banked high with papers, books
Every which way. I sat
On granite hearth, and your ideas
Sparked a transformation
Designed by Classical Theory.
They still envelop me like a cloak.
Compassion married to politics
Embrace heart and head and soul.

And I remember the little things.
Bounding up the stairs
At midnight. "It's a boy!"
Playing games with Richard
Guessing the Queen of Puddings.

Padding over Cobbles
Past the Campanile, the Rubrics.
The stairs up No. 40
Surely bore your imprint
Impressed there
On generations of students.

And I remember the night
You walked home from Trinity.
A car must wait
For tuition, bed and board.
All these things you gave
Unstintingly.

Down the years I hope
My children will remember
What I tell them. Of generosity
Of kindness, of my gratitude.
Such things should be remembered.

Valentine Urie, 1990

A couple of years after Don died, Daphne gave a sermon on Bereavement in Rathmichael Church, in which she spoke of her sadness, her loneliness, and her grief experiences. Of her sermons this is the one that has been best remembered.

Bereavement

Rathmichael
1992

'Blessed are they that mourn, for they shall be comforted.'

I hope you will be tolerant if I am personal in this address. In doing so, I take a little courage from the fact that the director of a communication course I attended some years ago advised us to base our preaching, as far as possible, on our own experience, and often as well on what was of concern to us at that particular time. The question of bereavement dominates my life at present, so I would like to share with you a little of what has been happening to me during the past two years of my husband's illness and death. I hope it may possibly be a little help to someone. It is also a form of thanks for the support and understanding I have received from this parish and the wider community. I had a clear insight during my first few weeks of grief, when a voice, as it were welling up from my unconscious it seemed, said, 'The future is going to be awful, but you will be supported.' So it has proved, beyond all my expectation and reasonable hope.

Perhaps you could count being cut off from my close Canadian family for my adult life as a form of bereavement; otherwise, until recently, I have been remarkably immune. This meant I had only second-hand knowledge of the difficulties which may be all too familiar to many of you. You will know about the empty chair and the all-pervading, empty silence at home. There is no one to share in the little bits of gossip and the private jokes of a lifetime. I could say that life has lost its flavour. But so often, when I have been on the brink of despondence, I have been rescued by some kindness, perhaps a phone call or a letter, or a special handshake, anything which reassures me that I am not forgotten.

When Jesus spoke about comfort for those who mourn, he may have been recalling Joseph's death and his mother's grief, but also remembering how her extended family and the close rural community centred on Nazareth had helped her. He would have been familiar with the words from Isaiah, 'a garland instead of ashes, a mantle of praise instead of fainting.' That is the kind of praise I can still experience from the natural beauty of flowers and landscape, and from the joy of friendship. That verse from R. L. Stevenson's *A Child's Garden of Verses* has often come to my mind to rescue me from depression:

> The world is so full of a number of things,
> I'm sure we should all be as happy as kings.

Consolation comes to different people in different ways. For me, it has been the very unexpected realisation that Donald's and my relationship has not come to a full stop, but is still developing, and has made progress since his death. I believe if he returned now, we would have a deeper affinity. This absolutely staggers me, and has exceeded all my expectations and imaginings. At the time of acute grief, my first concern was, of course, that he should be well cared for, and that he should not suffer pain or agitation.

But, as well, there was my own great sadness as I watched him being taken away from me. I did not know how I could face the months and years of separation, when I would have no contact with him, or even a glimpse of what his new life would be like. I tried reading the funeral service, but it did not meet my need. You know, we are told in the Bible to 'take no thought for the morrow, for the morrow will take thought for the things of itself.' But the prayer book speaks of having 'thankful remembrance of thy great goodness in past years,' and 'the hope in sure expectation of a happy reunion in the heavenly places.' That took care of the past and the future, but when Donald had gone, I would be between the past and the future, so how was I to face each day?

There has been an answer. It came to me quietly and gradually in the weeks after he died. As I have said, I began to be aware that a small part of me was still sharing time with him, even if it was on an intangible level, and was hard to put into words. More surprisingly still, I realised that he is helping me on this earthy and earthly plane which I must still inhabit. When I told a friend about this surprising development, she suggested it was God's way of meeting my special need. My role seems to be to cherish this insight, to do nothing which harms it, such as grumbling or feeling sorry for myself. And I must not give in to that most insidious thought, 'What is the use of going on?' If we are still in touch, and sharing, then I must do my bit. A widow I know, who was facing the loss of her husband and two sons in a boating accident some time ago, told me later that her husband was a constant help to her in bringing up their remaining children. I remember thinking, 'That is wonderful for her, but I am afraid it is too simple for me!' She repeated the sentiment after Donald's death. By that time I had become simple, too, and I understood what she meant. I should add that since then I have been given help by Donald in several difficult situations.

In view of what I have been saying, you will realise that whatever doubts I may have had in the past about future life, and personal survival after death, have evaporated. I find the words 'eternal life' full of meaning. By 'eternal life,' I refer to the life which should begin here and now, the kind of life which is characteristic of God, who is the creator and lover of beauty, the source of light and love and compassion, all the qualities shown in the life of Jesus Christ. If we give space and encouragement to this vision of eternal life, we are promised that it will grow in us here and now, and perhaps take us a little nearer to what we dimly think of as the Kingdom of

God. We are reminded of it in the words at Holy Communion: 'The body and blood of Christ keep you in eternal life.' This assumes we are already on that journey.

There is one other experience I would like to share with you. I have had just one dream about Donald since he died. It was a very personal and utterly consoling encounter. On reflection, the setting was not a place of flowers or even of music, as I might have expected, knowing his great love of both. Instead, he appeared to be on a pilgrim's way. I sensed he was trying to allay my feelings of isolation by including me. So is there still pilgrimage in heavenly places? Certainly I have never been able to think of Donald sleeping while the rest of us struggle on here; that would be out of character. 'Called to higher service,' but in some kind of comradeship with us, seems a more appropriate description.

Some hymns have begun to mean more to me in the last year. One of them is 'Lead kindly Light' by John Henry Newman. It is not very suitable for congregational singing, but I would like to conclude my remarks with the last two lines:

> and with the morn those angel faces smile,
> which I have loved long since and lost awhile.

There is no doubt that Daphne felt very much isolated from family after Don died. She travelled, but it became more difficult to do so with each passing year. Her friends were dying, which increased her feelings of loss. Her sisters had their own commitments and were elderly, too. Three of her children lived and worked in England and in Canada. About her grandchildren, she wrote, sadly, 'I'm destined to be an absentee grandmother.' Children and grandchildren did their best to visit when they could, and Daphne enjoyed a special relationship with her granddaughter, Joanna Wormell. Even when she felt lonely, Daphne would say, as she had years before, that she herself had made the decision to stay on in Ireland, and not to return to her native Canada, and not to try settling in London, and that there should be no feelings of guilt consequently.

Stephen was the one who lived nearby and who was a constant support and presence, even if their relationship was not always smooth. Stephen's marriage to Valerie was perhaps the happiest event of Daphne's widowhood. Her delight on this occasion helped to create the atmosphere that led to comments from guests, such as 'That was the happiest wedding I've ever been to' and 'A true celebration.'

Unbeknownst to Daphne, when she was eighty, Stephen set up a daily 'Daphne Check' system, where there would always be someone dropping in for some reason every day. For those of us far away, this gave great comfort.

In 1995, after attending a Trinity Week function in TCD, she wrote: 'Trinity Week is full of echoes from the past, and I escaped home to my garden as quickly as I could.'

In 1993 Professor R. J. A. Wilson, currently Head of the Department of Classical, Near Eastern and Religious Studies at the University of British Columbia, wrote the following:

> A most happy occasion took place on Friday 12th November 1993, when the Classical Society library in the School of Classics was formally renamed 'The Donald Wormell Room', in memory of the man who instilled in so many generations of TCD classicists a love and knowledge of Latin literature. The Provost, who became Donald Wormell's successor as Professor of Latin in 1978, spoke warmly of Donald's inspiring teaching and his qualities of Ciceronian *humanitas*, which won for him such a special place in the affections of his friends, colleagues and pupils. A splendid photograph of Donald has been hung in the room, and an elegant glass-fronted bookcase has been made to house the books which the Wormell family have most kindly donated from Donald's library for the use of undergraduates. A special bookplate has been designed, and affixed in each of these books. It was particularly fortunate that several members of the Wormell family were able to be present, including Daphne and sons Richard, Robin and Stephen, as well as several of Donald's friends and pupils and (as Donald would have wished) representatives of the present generation of TCD Classics students. The occasion was followed by a convivial dinner on Commons.

In her eighties, Daphne bought a computer, determined to master a tool that could bring her offspring closer. It was rough going for her. 'Why should I click on "Start" when I want to stop?' she would ask. Mostly she managed with patient assistance from neighbours, especially long-time family friend, Michael Ganly.

Daphne had been a conscientious housekeeper, keeping meticulous records of activities and finances in numerous notebooks. It was surprising to hear her on tape, in her eighties, say forcefully, 'I have always had the utmost difficulty in keeping the house, even to this day. I don't step into it rightly. I hate it. I hate having those restrictions or conditions, of having to do it, having to keep house. Housekeeping is a terrible strain.' Whenever she felt down or restricted, Daphne would know feelings of depression could be lurking around the corner. She now lived in an empty house, commitments were at their lowest, and her feelings of loneliness, sadness and loss of companionship took their turn in leading her to face depression. She countered these by taking in a lodger on weeknights. Brian Williams shared many breakfasts with Daphne, the two of them sitting in the kitchen nook, discussing ideas and events over their coffee. This helped focus her day ahead.

In her study, set up by the armchair, she kept a framed poem sent to her by her friend Cherry Dowrick. [The poem, *Alone*, is given on page 128]. She would read it as she sat alone in the evenings.

ALONE?

However lengthy or brief
the absence may have been,
always to be faced,
the return to the empty house!
The long path to my door
I tread with uncertainty;
key in lock ... I almost turn
and run. But where?

No escape – there is none.
What is on one's path must be faced,
understood; part of the picture
put in perspective.
What joy **has** been, still exists
in a different time zone,
like matter is indestructible,
although less tangible.

Unspoken, but deeply felt,
my prayerful request is
that the presence of God
may meet me there in my home,
as I cross the threshold,
transmuting pain to joy,
restoring my faith and strength
of purpose in life's pilgrimage.

Muriel E. Critoph.
The Friend, January 1998
Reproduced here by kind permission of Alena Critoph,
daughter of Muriel

13

THE WORMELL FAMILY

There were four of us Wormell kids, a common number in the post-war period. Boy, girl, boy, boy. You'd think I would have been spoilt, but it was one of Daphne and Don's parenting ideas that no favouritism be shown. They stuck to it well. And I don't believe they leaned more towards one of us over the others.

Richard arrived first, in 1943. Although caught up by events resulting from the war, Daphne and Don were leading peaceful, calm, quiet lives. If they were at home alone together, they would have been reading and discussing poetry. A good birthday present would have been a book of poetry, perhaps discovered in a second-hand bookstore.

Richard exploded onto the scene. He was bright, active, quick, noisy and mischievous. We know today that this personality in a child will lead to a gregarious adult whose company others will seek. But, in the forties, the general feeling was that Richard was out of control, and that Daphne and Don knew nothing about parenting. At two, he broke free on a bus, ran to the front from where he announced to all, 'I'm Richard, and I'm going to travel 'round the big, wide world.' These days he would be considered self assured and imaginative, and would be encouraged, but in the forties it caused only exasperation and exhaustion. Sent a toy cowboy pistol from Canada when five, he rushed to the pram, jammed it into a younger brother's mouth, and declared, 'Bang! Bang!

I'm going to shoot you dead.' One time the front door bell rang and Richard raced to be the one to open the door. 'Is your mother available?' the visitor enquired. 'Oh no, no', declared Richard. 'Not available. She is in the kitchen making sloe gin.' Without TV, it was a source of amazement as to where he got such ideas.

A cousin from Canada came to live with us for a year when Richard was twelve. They got up to hijinks, some unknown to Daphne and Don. They rode on their bikes all over Dublin, wild and free, and basically out of control. It was decided Richard should 'be sent away' to boarding school, to Campbell College, in Northern Ireland. Today, he says it was 'the making of him', but for the three siblings left behind, we lost out on sharing experiences with him through those teenage years. Before starting university, he spent a long summer in Canada, working with survey crews out of Calgary. He would have liked to have stayed longer, but he had been awarded an Entrance Scholarship to Trinity (ranking ninth out of all examinees), and he needed to return. Later, when Richard finished university, he worked in England, again away from the core of the family.

I was born in 1946. There was no space left for a second child, except to sit there, bob my long blond curls and bat my eyelashes. Why would I try to talk? Richard did enough for us both. I smiled, and that got attention, especially from visitors. No further effort was required. Was it any wonder that I appeared shy? And perhaps I was even a bit slow? I was badly bullied in the early school days, so I learned to stay very quiet, very still, unnoticed.

It was when Richard left and I went to Park House School that I began to come through. Not so pretty anymore, I could do well instead at sports, in drama and in music. Schoolwork was mostly a bother. I played with my younger brothers and their friends in the large backyard. 'Julia, you go in goal. We need to practise shooting.' 'Julia, we need to improve our rugger tackling. You run as fast as you can.' I would be bruised, but it was fun, and I made a great field hockey goalie on the senior team at school. When the coach discovered my skills, she asked, 'Where have you been?' 'With my brothers,' I replied.

Our parents were keen not to put pressure on us in any way – not academically, not socially and not with the chores. Daphne felt she had been over-burdened as a child, and was determined not to impose. Don felt he had been relentlessly pressured. A common saying of his to Daphne was, 'Leave them alone to find their own way.' I could have done with more pushing, especially academically. I did help take care of the sixty or more hens and bantams before and after school, and on weekends, but I loved being outside, so these duties were hardly tasks.

Robin came in 1949. To the delight of Richard, the third child was a second boy. A quieter, more serious child, his expressions were those of Daphne, but his temperament and his successes in sports, in academics, and in music were very much like those of his father. Robin studied Classics at Trinity, and on completing his degree, changed course and did Medicine. He practises in London, and recently received a Master of Science Degree in Sports Medicine, from Queen Mary and Westfield College, University of London.

The last child, Stephen, born in 1951, was also an achiever in all areas, most particularly in every sport in which he showed interest. More outgoing than Robin, he had high energy and a huge sense of fun. Robin and Stephen complemented each other well. They never fought, they had mutual friends, went to the same schools and participated in the same activities. After living for a while in England, Stephen is the only one to have settled in Dublin.

Parenting was a deadly serious undertaking for Daphne. All of us were heavily into sports, riding our bicycles down and back up that mountainside. Our appetites were large, and our health and welfare were a major concern. Taking great care with our diet, she ensured that we grew up strong and vigorous. We were encouraged to run wild and free in the fresh Sandyford air, which blew up from the sea or down from the Dublin and Wicklow mountains.

Family summer holidays were a major event, spanning all of August every year. Off we would go with half the kitchen's pots and pans, bicycles for everyone, stores of food from Don's vegetable garden, and games, cards and books for evening fun. In early years, everything, followed by everyone, was piled into the back of our greengrocer's van. Only a couple of hours' drive and we would have arrived in Blessington, where we holidayed near the reservoir. Mid-fifties saw us rattling in a railway carriage without sides or doors, on the track described by Percy French in 'Are you right there, Michael?' on the way to a Kilkee summer house. I remember it being dark, the cold wind blasting our faces, the bicycles sliding ever closer to the open sides, and hoping that the journey would never end. Don was laughing, invigorated by it all, and saying over and over how perfect it was.

In later years we had a car that could pull a trailer, but the trouble was that the vehicle was a Morris Minor and we had all grown big. So Richard would be sent on ahead, riding his bicycle. Daphne and Don sat in the front of the car, everyone else, including our Nannie, was jammed into the back. The dog was under our feet, and all the goods were in the trailer. It took us all day to get to Roundstone, or to Skibbereen, but we sang and carried on to pass the time.

How I loved those trips, and how I hated September as the countdown of days to the next summer holiday had to begin all over again. It was small wonder when I had little ones myself that I loved to bring them over for holidays by the Irish seaside, for once again Daphne would manage the whole event. On one of these, while driving to Donegal, I put on the tape recorder. Don recounted classical myths and legends to our two open-mouthed boys, and Daphne explained about each ruin as we sped by. With her incredible memory, no matter where in Ireland we were, she could recount the dates, what had happened there, who had lived there, to whom they were related today, and why it was now uninhabited.

Daphne and Don had both spent student years far from home. Although they knew how lonely that could be, and how difficult it could be to make social contacts, they had also experienced some generous hospitality. They were determined to do the same for others. They opened their house gladly and with warmth to undergraduate student gatherings. Professors, lecturers, and graduate students would fill out the ranks. These student parties at Gatineau became famous – for marvellous cooking, for Don's special punch and for the variety of guests one would encounter. Preparations took days to complete. Furniture would be removed from the living room and the dining room to make space. Pies, tarts, cakes, squares would be baked. On the night of the party Don would mix the punch, again and again, in a giant tub in a room off the kitchen. It was a delight for us youngsters to watch the bottles gurgle and the pop fizz as the concoction was prepared. Daphne undertook mixing the crowd, making sure all were acquainted. Several couples, thus introduced, later married. Our job was to pass around plates laden with food through crowded rooms and hallways. We could tell when a student was living on a meagre allowance, for he or she would devour the food. Of course, all of the students would be thirsty all of the time, and soon the party was in full spin. When everyone was occupied, we kids would head into the punch room and help ourselves to a glass or two, taken in one gulp. It was a good way for children to learn about alcohol.

Many visitors came and went, from every continent. As Fred Appelbe said in his eulogy for Daphne, years later, 'Gatineau became an oasis of reckless hospitality for family, friends, staff and multitudes of hungry and thirsty students. The Prof. and his Missus welcomed all and sundry with glowing warmth.'

14

NANNIE

Daphne's fear of succumbing to depression was high when her children were young, a time when she was tied to the house. To help her cope, Daphne consulted a psychiatrist. He told her she was an extrovert, needing to socialise, needing to get out of the house. His strongest advice to her was to hire some live-in help. There were several maids and mother's helpers that came and went over the early years, most notably Kitty Keating, up from the country, near Arklow. Kitty's brother, Jim, was already doing some of the heavy digging in the garden on Saturdays. As he cycled home to Barnacullia from work on the other side of the River Liffey on Friday evenings, he would know if he was needed in the garden on Saturday if a rock was placed on top of the gatepost. His wife, Sarah, would accompany him to help with cleaning the house. The Keatings were special to us, but it was Kitty that enthralled Don with her intelligent conversation as he dried the dishes for her every evening after dinner. In the early fifties, Kitty left us, was happily married and became a mother herself.

The Dowrick family, living in Kilternan at the time, had a mother's help, but Frank, a Trinity lecturer in Law, and his wife, Cherry, had decided that they were going to try to manage without one. Bella Napier from Bray was now available, and came highly recommended. She was interviewed. Daphne could see the gold before her, but Bella was not so sure that three wild boys and a girl just as bad were what she wanted. She returned to the Dowricks to say the position would not be suitable for her. Cherry Dowrick assured and cajoled, and it was eventually agreed that Bella would come to Gatineau for a three-week trial period. Daphne and Don were going to Copenhagen for a holiday, and the two eldest children would be away, staying with friends. Daphne's aunt, Vera Murphy, daughter of Vice-Provost Goligher, came out to stay with Bella to help manage things. Vera was persuasive, and by the time Daphne and Don returned home, Bella had had a change of heart.

Bella would have her own bedroom, would wear a uniform and would be given the title of 'Nannie'. She would help with the cooking and light cleaning, do the laundry, ironing and sewing, and look after the children. Of course, this expanded into every area – Nannie did gardening, helped with the care of over sixty chickens, and the selling of their eggs. She was a first-rate nurse, was steady in a crisis and was Daphne's right-hand girl in all household matters. It was clear that Daphne and Don would take care of the discipline, and would make all major decisions. But Nannie answered the doorbell and the telephone, and she sat as a member of the family at the dining room table.

Getting up at seven and after her early morning cup of tea, Nannie would polish all the shoes required for that day. She next woke up the household, prepared breakfast and got the children organised. She would work hard all day, and for that she had two afternoons off, Sunday and Thursday. She received five pounds pay per week, as well as her pension stamps paid. That was a good enough deal in those days. Nannie was content to live with only a few personal possessions. Blessed with an even temperament, rarely becoming upset or annoyed, she frequently laughed and carried on. Occasionally, we managed to reverse the tables, and tease her. On Saturday afternoons, she baked stacks of cookies and cakes. These would be spread out to cool on racks. It was forbidden food. One of us would ring the front doorbell, and as Nannie made her way through the hall to answer the bell, we ran in by the back door and grabbed fistfuls of the goodies. She would laugh at our ingenuity.

In 1960, Nannie was hospitalised for a gall bladder operation, which was followed by a recuperation period of over a month. Years later, Daphne was to say that during that time she 'nearly went mad' trying to keep the house and family running smoothly. The lives of these two women were interwoven, each depending on the other. However, all those who worked for Daphne soon became devoted to her, keeping in touch with her to the end. In later years,

Nannie said, 'Mrs Wormell is now like a mother to me.'

The most striking part of Nannie's time at Gatineau was how well she was received by everyone. All visitors held her in high esteem. She was considered family by everyone who met her, and it seemed that all of our Dublin society knew and cared about Nannie. Politicians, clergy, academics, students – all loved her greeting them at the door, or on the telephone, and all called her Nannie. By religion she was Catholic, but from Archbishop George Simms to Vice-Provost Herbert Parke, from Northrop Frye to Lady Plowden, she was considered a major part of the family fabric, always deserving and receiving full credit.

Even when the children had long gone, there was still lots for Nannie to do, helping Daphne in an even wider variety of ways. In June 1974, in her annual report as Chairperson of the Irish Pre-School Playgroups Association, Daphne acknowledged 'Mrs Roberts and her helper, Miss Napier, who have come along each month and so quietly and reliably looked after tea arrangements.' Nannie would have baked many goodies the week before, would have been happy to listen to discussions on bringing up young children, and would have then served the tea, smiling all the while.

There is no doubt that having Nannie at the helm for over forty years freed Daphne from overbearing duties. Sound steerage meant schedules would be kept, the children would be cared for after school, a nutritious dinner would be on the table in time and evenings would be free for studying, writing, and consultations with Don.

15

HOME AT GATINEAU FROM 1949

Daphne had all three: self-discipline, drive and determination. They were a part of everything she did. When spring-cleaning, carpets would be hung outside and bashed with a bamboo carpet beater. Not one dust particle would escape her. When it was fruit-picking time, the current and gooseberry bushes would be assaulted. Family members would be swept up and energised alongside. Excursions to the giant blackberry bushes in the hedges and fields behind our house led to baskets and bowls laden with large, succulent berries. After hours of prickles and orange tawny spider bites, after carrying heavy loads home, the talk and thrust of the following week would be jam-making. The deep pantry shelves would be packed with the most delicious jams ever tasted, all in carefully labelled jars.

Unaware of the energy she expended, when she sat down for lunch Daphne would frequently comment on how tired she was. Nannie would catch our eye, raise her own heavenwards and say, 'Mrs Wormell, you never stop.' Always taking an hour's nap right after lunchtime, it was her quiet time. In the summer she would curl up on a small rug in the long, cool grass, somewhere out in the garden. She would take *The Listener* to read, for stimulation. If she fell asleep while holding it, it would quietly fall to the floor or the ground. She loved to wake to a fresh cup of tea. I was happy to be the bearer, even if it was a tricky balancing act, carrying a tray with teapot, cups and saucers, milk, a plate of bread and butter and searching for her in what seemed to me to be a meadow. 'Would you like the bread?' she would enquire. Relaxed and perhaps having had a dream of things past, she would talk about whatever first came into her head. Frequently, this would be about her family in Canada or earlier generations in Ireland. She laid the seeds of a passion for family history.

If Daphne was at home in the evening, she would go to bed early, finally worn out. We all knew for certain that come the next morning, she would be ready to go again. The most striking feature of her drive was how quietly it all happened. There were no explosions, no whirlwinds. She could stop on wash days, Mondays and Thursdays, surrounded by mounds of smelly socks, which she herself always washed by hand, or by piles of dirty, cotton sheets waiting for Nannie and the wringer washer. She would perch on a stool in the kitchen, calm and alert, have a cup of tea and heartily laugh at a funny incident, or something that someone had said. If the phone rang in the middle of her cleaning out the cinders from a fireplace, she would quietly wipe her hands on a rag, sit on a stool and lift the receiver. She was able to do two or three things at one time, and think of as many other items at the same time.

It might appear to someone looking in that Daphne did little in the house, leaving most of the daily work to others. There is no doubt that Nannie worked hard, but Daphne did as much. Daphne would say, 'I have no right to ask Nannie to do messy tasks.' On a Saturday, Daphne would be up early, rotating clothes and linen in and around the clothes airing cupboard. After breakfast she would clean out the chickens, preparing them for the Sunday dinner table. She might then wash her hands so she could have a morning coffee with a friend who had dropped in. After this break, she could be found brushing down and polishing the stairs, for what use was the large hoover on a staircase? Next she would scrub the kitchen floor, which would take an hour and a half. It was a daunting task to scrub and wash that marble floor. One time when I was about 10 I tried to 'be helpful' and when adults weren't looking, I persuaded Sandra Ganly (*née* Johnstone) to join in on cleaning that floor. We must have tired after half an hour, for we tried to hurry up the process by swishing half a dozen full buckets of water across the floor. This became known as 'Julia's flood'.

In the summer, Daphne's energy centred on preserving fruit and jam-making. The whole family would be advised of the picking times: 'Red currants this afternoon. Blackberries with picnic all day tomorrow.' Down in the garden there were bushes of red currants, black currants, gooseberries and raspberries.

Loganberries grew profusely over the long garden fence. Trees were laden with apples and pears. In the fields on all sides were blackberries and crab apples. Giant tubs of picked fruit were in every corner, and as many vats of fruit being processed sat on the counters. Piles of boxes with jars waiting to be sterilised would appear from the attic. The shelves of the pantry soon became laden with hundreds of jars, all filled and all perfectly labelled by year and content. When marmalade-making season arrived, it all began again with tubs of sliced oranges, chopped lemons and grapefruits. We would do our homework those evenings to the sound of the pound scales clattering and the sugar being poured out of bags into the weighing bowls. Daphne and Nannie worked efficiently, side by side, but it was Daphne who got in the supplies, did much of the cooking, and who organised the day's activities.

If Daphne and Don were going out socially in the evening, around 6 p.m. Don would begin to worry about getting out on time. Daphne was frequently late. He would ask Nannie, 'Have you seen Herself?' On finding her, 'We need to leave in about an hour,' he would say. On hearing those words, I would head up to their bedroom. Daphne was thrilled that I was expressing an interest. I was entranced by the smell of her perfume, the sound of her gown swishing and the glitter of her jewellery. She would say, 'One day you will be going out like this,' and, when I was older, 'I feel guilty that I'm the one going out, it should be you.' Don would help her on with her coat, smile, bend to kiss the vision before him, and take her out to the car. I would climb back up the stairs to their room, sit on the side of the bed and smell the perfume in the air. I was always content to be the one staying at home, not having to go out trying to be witty, clever and charming.

The same energy glows from her diaries and notebooks. As a young teenager she was running the family home in Calgary. As we have seen, she milked the cow before breakfast and got her four siblings fed and dressed and out to school, before she thought of her own day. Eva, her mother, was in bed struggling with thyroid deficiencies and had even suffered a bout of typhoid, which she contracted from the drinking water. Daphne's sister, Val, recalled lying awake late in the night, straining to catch what Eva was saying as she sat on Daphne's bedside in the dark, telling her eldest daughter of Ireland and of her family back home in the old country.

Daphne's childhood diary was written at night, frequently after her light was supposed to be out. Each entry has paragraphs telling of her great fatigue, and how she struggled against it. The family moved from Ottawa, where Daphne had been her happiest as a child, back to Calgary. She was now an outsider at school, had few friends, for all her dear ones were back in Ottawa. She was frequently mocked and teased. She hated it.

At the same time, she was struggling against her father and his Victorian Dublin ways. He believed if a girl stayed out after sunset she would get pregnant. Daphne had to be home before dark, and was not permitted out again that evening. It gets dark before 4 pm in Calgary in the winter months. All social events were therefore not allowed. Wrestling with duty versus sociability, with right against wrong, with her father's strictures and her mother's tears at seeing her daughter so torn, the stress took its toll. These struggles would haunt her all her life, for she was never reconciled with her father. He died while she was a student at Trinity. She was still talking about it at age 85.

For Daphne, her teenage years consisted of being exhausted, having low self-esteem, being the cause of upsets between her parents, having responsibilities beyond her years and even being the disciplinarian of her youngest siblings. Resentment from them for the spankings and scoldings she inflicted, lasted a lifetime. She was parenting as a child. It was too much. For the rest of her life, she feared and fled from 'feeling flat and internally bruised.' She would refer to it quietly as her depression. 'Warding off depression with routine,' she would note. 'Easy to get depressed if you don't set about your tasks purposefully', or 'Need for discipline of time, early in the day.' Common themes in her diaries are: 'If you do too much, alas! the only thing is to be strictly methodical' and 'One day I realised my list required priorities.' She could discuss these issues with one of her mother's sisters-in-law, Vera Murphy, who told her, 'To avoid depression, do not let yourself reminisce.'

Daphne's sisters considered Daphne, even as a child, to have a spiritual aura about her. They said she inherited it from her mother, that it was always there, a part of her deeper self. I recall a number of times when I would burst open the door into the living room to practise the piano, to find my mother sitting alone in a comfortable chair. She would look as if she was asleep, but in fact she was having a quiet time, a prayerful time. My piano playing would speedily send her out of the room, on to the next task.

Daphne wrote this entry in her diary shortly after returning to Dublin to study at Trinity College:

Wednesday, October 27th, 1937

It's strange that, in this old-worldly city of Dublin, I should find it so hard to get even a fleeting glimpse of that idealism that used to come so often in radiant moments. Here, it seems that the atmosphere is already set, that the only effort is to manage to be born into a comfortable life! Where are those great visions of Nature, with her soothing balm, and her cleansing winds? I know they must be somewhere just beyond my reach, because surely if there is a still, small voice in the Glen, that voice should be infinitely sweeter in the mystical atmosphere of Ireland. I looked out of the window one night and saw the moon, clean and pure and independent, above the squalor, the dirt, and that sense of inevitability which pervades Dublin, and I could feel its magnetic power lifting me out of circumstances for a moment, and showing me 'the larger view of God'. Then when Turner Layton[6] played, a surging desire to excel in something nearly overwhelmed me, but one is soon chained again to the ground by the clown who catches balls in the baskets on his back.

When Daphne began studying History in Trinity, fellow student Rose Gwynn found her 'reserved and serious, more mature than we were and with that gentle Canadian voice which in itself made her a special person. Her round eyes seemed to find us frivolous – which indeed we were – and she set an example of study which gave me pause for thought.' Daphne wrote about this time 'If I have an idle evening I feel guilty about it.'

As had happened to Eva, Daphne's thyroid was affected, and never recovered. The most striking symptom for her was the loss of her hair at different times in her life. This was devastating for a young woman, before there were wigs other than theatrical versions. If she and Don were going out to a dinner party, or to an event in Trinity, she would tie a scarf over her head, upside down, fastening it with a knot on the top. It would be obvious she was bald, but she would be serene. She had done the best she could, and she was determined to go on.

She lost her hair around pregnancies. Waking up one morning after her first child was born, she found much of her hair on the pillow. It would grow back in fits and starts, only to thin out again. Unlike today, bald heads were rarely seen. World War II was very fresh in people's minds, and bald heads were connected to concentration camps. Eventually, wigs became fashionable and affordable, first from North America, and finally in Ireland. She learned to cope well at each step. Occasionally, as we all gathered in the hallway to go out together as a family, she would have slipped her wig on incorrectly. Don would gently say, 'Daphne, your

---

6   Turner Layton was a singer, composer and pianist who lived from 1892 to 1953. With Henry
   Creamer he co-wrote the popular song 'After You've Gone.'

hair is backwards.' 'Is it?' she would ask with a laugh as she glanced in the mirror, deftly twisting it back, right way up.

Having afternoon tea on the back lawn in the summer sunshine, she would slip off her wig. 'It's like wearing a heated rug on your head,' she would say. 'And the midges have got under and are biting.' We were well used to it. The great fear for us all was that a visitor would come around the house on the garden path and discover Daphne in her baldness. 'Let me know if someone's coming,' she would say, lying down on a spread-out blanket. It was a matter of great pride and honour to warn her speedily and quietly. The whispered words 'Someone's coming,' one of us lifting up a jumper, or a tea-towel, or rushing to intercept the visitor – anything to give Daphne a moment to pull on her wig securely. Then the guest would be given a welcome like nowhere else. I used to wish *I* could be a visitor, just once, to the Wormell household so that I could be greeted with such genuine warmth and cordiality.

Nannie came rushing out one time, saying, 'Mrs Wormell, there are tinkers coming in through the gate!' Daphne quietly got up, telling Nannie that she would deal with them. The doorbell rang and Daphne opened the front door to a crowd. She stood there, smaller than any of them, put up her hand and pulled off her wig. 'Oh, be Jesus! Lord help us!' was all they could say, as they fled out through the gate in horror. We had no more doorbells rung by gypsies for years after.

Daphne had been visiting a friend who had had a baby in a Nursing Home in Earlsfort Terrace. It was raining. Having put up her umbrella, she made her way back to her car. Almost there, a woman rushed up to her, saying, 'Hey! You! Would yez move yerself on. This is my bloody beat!' Startled, Daphne jerked her umbrella upwards to get a better look. One of the umbrella's ribs became caught in her wig, lifting it off her head. The prostitute ran off in fright. Daphne was still laughing when she arrived home.

Daphne worried that she had little sense of humour. She would have been amazed that she is fondly remembered for 'her great laugh', and her humorous story-telling.

In the 1950 edition of 'The Irish Housewife', published by the Irish Housewives Association, Daphne contributed an article titled 'Hold Back That Clock.' In the final paragraph she states: 'It seems we are destined in the modern world to have our hands full all the time. Past, present and future: I have rushed, I am rushing, and I am about to rush. Sometimes I think it would be very restful to be a grandmother; but that is putting the clock forward, and I am only too anxious to hold it back.'

16

TEACHING, WRITING AND INFLUENCING

Daphne thought of herself as a 'Child of the Depression', referring to her childhood during the Depression years in Canada. Notes to be mailed to children or grandchildren, and later, prayers to be read out in Church services, were written on saved pieces of paper. She preferred stiffer quality paper, similar to that used for plain, white postcards. Always conserving, she used old calling cards from her mother's collection, or squares with a TCD logo on one side. For example, she wrote 'A prayer for the clergy and especially our Rector' on one such piece. On turning it over, one finds printed:

WOMEN'S TEA CLUB
Trinity College, Dublin
The next meeting will be held
on
in No. 6

R.S.V.P.
to the honorary secretary
6 Trinity College
Tea, 4.15 p.m.   Dublin

She wrote to me when I had been granted citizenship of Canada. On one side, in her handwriting, it says:

For Julia – As one Canadian to another: Welcome to the Club!!
Aim: To look upwards and outwards and keep interests wide and lively.

Turn over the slip of paper, and there printed, in the centre, is:

With the Compliments of the Vice-Provost.

Although she was never wealthy, to live with Daphne was to live with great richness. Everyone in her household tried hard to keep up with her as she ricocheted along, involved as she was in so many areas at different periods of her life.

She sat on the Editorial Board of the Irish Housewives Association. She wrote articles for 'The Irish Housewife', the annual magazine that was published by that Association. Her articles were varied, from 'Hold Back That Clock' in 1950, to 'Prices : Protection : Progress' in 1952.

In the 1950s Daphne taught English History, Ancient History, History of Art and Civics at Knockrabo School. On May 22nd, 1957, Headmistress Wiltshire wrote Daphne a reference, which in part says:

'Mrs. Wormell's culture and intelligence is such that she can interest the children in a wide range of subjects; she encourages discussion in her classes, and does much to widen the outlook of the children. On several occasions she has taken a party to visit the Dail or the National Gallery, which everyone has found a very interesting and valuable experience.

'Throughout her two years' connection with the school, Mrs. Wormell has been unfailingly reliable, always ready to co-operate with others, and a delightful colleague. As the school is closing at the end of the present term she will no longer be able to continue teaching here; I think any school would be lucky to have her assistance, and I shall always be glad to speak on her behalf.'

Daphne taught Secondary School History in Knockrabo, in Park House, and in Hillcourt. On returning from Princeton, where she had taken courses in Art Appreciation, she taught History of Art in The High School to a small group of boys who had expressed interest in the subject. Some former pupils have said they found her to be one of the best teachers they ever had. When we had no car she rode to the schools on her bicycle. In 1970–71 Daphne took up the challenge of taking the H. Dip. Ed. alongside her friend Katharine Liddle (*née* Gwynn). They had considered taking the Diploma for years, and by the time they signed on, the degree was becoming a requirement for teachers to hold a job. They wrote their exams in June. Three weeks before then, Daphne was sitting on a panel held at the Divinity Hostel to discuss the position of the curate and his wife. One week prior to exams she attended a talk on the State of the Church of England. Of the exams themselves, she wrote: 'The horrifying experience is over; my nightmare would be to be locked into Hut 1 for the rest of my life; I have been dwelling in cuckoo-land.' The day after the last exam she attended a Trinity Hall Committee meeting and the Playgroups AGM. Her teaching time was ending as other interests were taking over.

For a number of years Daphne provided instruction both in the classroom and on bus tours to groups of foreign students. Most of these were French, many were adults, and her knowledge of Irish history served her well. This could mean four mornings a week for a month. It would take most of her energy for that time.

In 1974, Daphne was invited by the Principal of Alexandra School and College to stand in for a curate who was going on holiday. Her assignment was to teach Church Doctrine. She wrote, 'I took up the challenge. The new school is very pleasant and the atmosphere in the staff-room is wonderful. I forgot I should wear a gown, but a teacher lent me hers. As for the girls, they are lively enough. We had a short discussion on euthanasia, and next week I'm to talk about baptism. What I welcome is a chance to find out what young people are thinking, about religion and church-going nowadays. It is already quite clear to me from students' remarks that the parents don't *ever* discuss religion with their families. One young girl proceeded to tell me she was the product of a mixed marriage. She said, 'My mother is Catholic and my father is Protestant, but they are both atheists.' She continued, 'But I'm not, I'm just taking time off to make up my own mind.' She related how her mother had had her baptised a Catholic, secretly, and that when her father found out he was 'raging', so he had had her secretly baptised a Protestant. Then it was my turn to say if that was so, she had in fact been baptised a *Christian* and that officially each church recognises the other's baptism. I hope I don't have the parents' wrath on my head!'

She sat on the Adult Education Council, as part of the Board of Education of the General Synod of the Church of Ireland, from its inception in 1973 until 1992.

Articles Daphne wrote were printed in *The Irish Times*, such as 'American dinner at eight' which describes dinner parties she attended while with Don when he was on sabbatical at the Princeton Institute in the States for the year 1967–1968. The last two paragraphs are as follows:

'American parties are shorter than ours, so often you leave about 10:30. You do bumps-a-daisy against the other guests as you put on your galoshes, then making sure that you have told everyone how pleased you are to have met them, you say a warm thank-you and a very quick goodbye, and get out of the door before the cold air from the North Pole has time to get in.

'One practical result for me is that I think I now have a better idea of what to serve Americans when they visit us. Perhaps a joint and roast potatoes; if not, braised steak or beef-steak-and-kidney pie, as our gravy is so much better. As for mixed grills, they have never heard of them. For dessert I'll certainly have trifle – almost unknown in the States and most popular. And I mustn't forget that Americans love our cider. Everything should be as tender as possible for people who put tenderness before flavour, but don't let's get upset if food is left at the side of the plate; that's only a part of the American way of life. Indeed we shouldn't worry too much at all. Americans are very informal and appreciative, and the really kind thing we can do is to feed them in our own homes. I know how much their invitations have meant to us.'

Other published articles ranged from 'Education in Canada' to one on a place in British Columbia called 'Spuzzum.' She appeared on the Radio Telefís Éireann program *Outlook* a number of times. This involved giving a 3½ minute talk on television late at night. Many Mothers' Union groups around the country invited her to give a talk to them on her thoughts about women in the home, parenting, Adult Education and women becoming ordained.

In 1968/9 she wrote a series of articles for 'The Church of Ireland Magazine', which was edited by Dr Kenneth Milne. She wrote on the main events of the Church calendar: Advent, Christmas, Lent, Easter, Whitsuntide. The Christmas article, titled 'Once in Royal David's City' finishes as follows:

If we read the Gospel narrative of the Nativity straight through we are given a vivid insight into what things are first with God. We learn that He does not respond to worldly might with a display of omnipotence, but with the utmost reticence and simplicity; that He has forever hallowed the ordinary events of humdrum daily life; and further (here the poetic symbols come into their own) that He has shown his favour to men of vision, whether these are shepherds, who share an earthy life with animals, or wise men, who live a kingly life seeking wisdom. Finally, it is the writers of the Gospels who convey to us the message of reconciliation that runs through the narrative and appeals to the whole of our personalities.

As the word 'holiday' suggests, days of break from work were once holy days, and it may have some little significance that 'whole' and 'holy' have the same derivation. Perhaps by striving to be whole and integrated people, not fragmented, in bits, blown this way and that, we may be moving a few steps along the road to holiness. Christmas appeals to our senses, our imagination, and our need for community; it speaks not of outworn symbols or dissipation of energy and thought, but of a lively renewal and knitting together. For what could be more whole than Jesus Christ, who is at the centre of this great festival, and who slipped into the world as a little child that we might be enabled to live as the children of God?

In the 'Easter' article, published in the April 1969 edition of the Magazine, we find the following:

It is evident from the Bible that those who saw the Risen Christ did so because they had the necessary vision, because they were spiritually mature. When He walked with his disciples He had manifested an imaginative style of life. We think of His poetic imagery and storytelling, His charismatic power of eliciting response as He moved graciously through the crowds. We use the word 'Grace' to describe the creative quality of life which hallows what it touches and it was an awareness of that graciousness in His Presence after death which seems to have aroused the disciples' response ... In the philistine society in which we live where artists are the poor relations it is all too easy to forget that faith is closely tied to the gifts of the imagination and that it is the prime duty of all who follow Christ to cultivate and encourage artistic expression.

Knowing there were many areas in which parents could work with young children to stimulate and encourage them, Daphne was acutely aware there was little material available to help young mothers. Of her own experiences as a mother she said, 'I knew I should have been doing things with the children to help them along, but I was at a loss as to what, and no-one else had any ideas, either.' Daphne's interest in Pre-School Playgroups was based on what had been her own desperate need as a mother for sound advice, and for play materials suitable for pre-schoolers. She worked to make available books for children to read, and to supply titles of books on parenting for their mothers. She felt young mothers needed support groups, should have explanations and answers to their queries, required demonstrations and, most of all, should be encouraged to take time-out to spend with their husbands. Daphne worked to bring in water-tables and sand-tables for the pre-schools. She arranged talks by visiting experts from the U.K., many of whom stayed at Gatineau.

Daphne was introduced to Elizabeth Moloney[7], who has this to say about what followed:

> I had already just started a small playgroup, and there were about ten others who also had groups. We thought we could start up an Irish Playgroups Association similar to one that had been set up in England, but we didn't know how to go about setting up an Association. How should we do it? What were the steps we needed to take? What were the legal requirements and the Government's requirements? What was our ethos? Did we need memoranda about setting up Playgroups? I was determined to get an Association organised and to build it on a good footing.
>
> I met Daphne and told her about this, and she said to me, "You can do it, and I'll come along with you." She was a marvellous person who opened up a whole world to me. She worked especially with Molly Walmsley and Maureen Hope. We set up a Committee in 1969, and we held a number of meetings among ourselves. We were full of enthusiasm. Daphne and Molly Walmsley would say they would stay for the business part of the meeting only and then they'd go off home, and the rest of us, the leaders, would stay on for hours, sometimes to 5:30 a.m., working out what we needed to do with the children.
>
> Daphne calmly and firmly knew where she was going with the Playgroups, how to set it all up and she always felt she was going to achieve that objective.

Daphne was instrumental in introducing many playgroups in Dublin, including one of the first workplace groups, the crèche in Trinity. She helped to build up the Pre-School Playgroups Association and was Chairperson for two years, 1972–74. In her address to the Annual General Meeting in May, 1973, she

7 The full text of the interview with Elizabeth Moloney is at Appendix 2

noted with pleasure that 'every Dublin newspaper since Christmas has had articles on the pre-school child.' She goes on to emphasise that all playgroups need support, and that playgroup leaders, and mothers and fathers, especially fathers, need encouragement, need to be more involved at every level, and should have the opportunity of education. 'Do parents know about playdough, children's painting, active play or how to set up a nature corner?' None of these had been available or even known to Daphne as a young mother, and were only emerging in the early 1970s. 'A deprived society is one that neglects its under-fives,' she declared. Her personal experience led her to say, 'The mother may have good reason to feel emotionally and physically exhausted.'

She was a long time member of the Dublin University Women Graduates Association, having been on the Executive as an undergraduate. Daphne was President in 1984–85, when Trinity was going through a period of unprecedented change with a vastly increased number of undergraduates, together with a chronic shortage of funds. Undismayed, she and her committee guided the Association gently but firmly with the aim of keeping in touch with the University and contributing, when appropriate, to life there. She started the DUWGA lunch on Trinity Monday which gives returning scholars more time to meet each other and the opportunity to include their partners in the day's celebrations. She reported with satisfaction on the activities of the Irish Federation of University Women, and welcomed its links with European and worldwide organisations. She found it rewarding that several university women from the States had got in touch with DUWGA when visiting Ireland.

Daphne loved the opportunity the meetings of the DUWGA provided for her to get together with friends and colleagues. With her close friend Joyce Craig (*née* McGilligan) she set up the poetry group, which continues to meet on Monday mornings. Sometimes a poet being studied came into the discussion group and participated. Seamus Heaney read poetry to the group on several occasions. One member of this group, Clarissa Pilkington, wrote an account of the group's foundation in verse, as follows:

An Account of Some Recent Activities of the D.U.W.G.A. 1984:

> Joyce and Daphne got the notion,
> And they put their plan in motion
> To drive away our Monday morning blues,
> That we'd meet to study Russian,
> Or to have a group discussion

On some topic that was current in the news.
But we came to the conclusion
That there was too much confusion
In the world for us to make our wishes known.
And Russian would defeat us –
Ev'n their alphabet would beat us –
So we had to think of something less high-flown.

Should we read some Irish verse?
Oh – in English, not in Erse!
Gerry Watts would guide our reading to begin with.
If we felt the need to sack her
There was Frances Gwynn to back her.
So here was a course of study we could win with.

Many learned things were said
As we spoke of what we'd read,
(We read Swift and Mangan, Ferguson and Synge).
There were erudite debates
On the politics of Yeats,
And on Kavanagh and Joyce our thoughts took wing.

At length we came to Heaney,
(He who wrote of Mad Sweeney),
And we read his poems and worshipped at his shrine.
He awoke our admiration
And we found exhilaration,
There was magic, there was music in each line.

There is no gauge that can measure
Our immense delight and pleasure
When he came, and read, of reason and of rhyme.
Well – that day is gone and past,
But the memory will last
For all of us until the end of time.

Francis Boyd took us "down under",
And displayed for us the wonder
Of native arts which Western man can't rival.
And though white men take their places
In that land of open spaces,
May the "Abos" win their struggle for survival.

In the Ulster poets' writing
We found much that was exciting –
Our ambition is to meet all of them one day.
Meanwhile you'll understand
When this devoted band
Of ladies tell you why they do like Monday.

Clarissa Pilkington

When in Princeton with Don during his sabbatical year to the Institute for Advanced Study, in 1967/8, Daphne became aware of, and then saw first hand, the work done by a relative in Cincinnati in the organising and running of a sale of second-hand books as a fund-raiser for charity. The idea stayed with Daphne. She had been a long-serving member of Trinity Trust. In 1989 she suggested to the TCD Association and Trust that graduates might like to contribute to Trinity's Quatercentenary fund-raising campaign by giving books for a book sale. Joyce Craig supported her proposal and helped Daphne to form a committee of staff and graduates, with Dr Eda Sagarra in the chair, Norah Kelso of the Association as secretary, and David Norris representing the Friends of the Library. Graduates were contacted and asked to give books for a sale to be held in the Exam Hall on 27th and 28th April, 1990. About 5,000 books were dropped off in Norah's office in East Theatre and were sorted, priced and boxed in the Graduates' Common Room. A Friday evening reception allowed graduates the first opportunity to buy books, and an auction, held on the Saturday morning, raised £2,500 of the final total of £9,400.

All proceeds were to go to the Library. The first Book Sale took place in April 1990, and, now firmly established as the annual TCD Association & Trust/Friends of the Library Book Sale, it is an annual event held in the Examination Hall. It has become an important occasion both in College and in Dublin life, drawing together staff, students and graduates to work for its success. Daphne wrote, 'It is quite amazing to see the long hours of effort that our volunteers contribute to the Book Sale. They are the reason why the Sale continues to be such a success.'

Charles Benson, Keeper of Early Printed Books in the Library, wrote to thank Daphne after the first sale:

> Trinity College Library Dublin
> Department of Early Printed Books
> 8th May 1990
>
> Dear Mrs Wormell,
>
> I would just like to congratulate you on the enormous success of your idea of a book sale. It has, I think, exceeded everybody's expectations. You will be delighted to hear that books are already coming in for next year's one.
>
> It was a most happy suggestion of yours, and the library will benefit greatly.
>
> Yours sincerely,
> Charles Benson

Ann Budd, who with others worked so closely and diligently developing the TCD Book Sale into what it is today, wrote: 'Those who witnessed Daphne's achievements had to watch carefully as she did everything without throwing her weight around. You didn't always realise where the project had started.'

The conviction that Daphne deserved an Honorary Degree from Trinity for her work for women resulted in her being awarded an Honorary MA, in 1996. The Public Orator, Dr J. V. Luce elegantly drew attention[8] to her work for Women in Ministry, as President of the Women Graduates Association and as the originator of the annual Book Sale. Trinity had publicly recognised the value of Daphne's work – and she was pleased. She said afterwards, 'I heard the words describing someone, and I looked around to see who they were talking about. Finally, I realised it was me.' Her appreciation of what had been said about her was heightened because her Donald had held the position of Public Orator for TCD before Dr Luce and Daphne knew the work that was involved in preparation of orations.

Daphne was a letter writer all her life. She learned the value of letters

---

[8]   The oration is recorded on pages 206–207 of Luce, J. V., *Orationes Dubliniensis Selectae II 1990–2002*, Hinds, 2004

received when she was torn from her good friends in Ottawa when her family went back west to Calgary. Her diaries, which she began at age thirteen and continued until she died, have in the margins lists of letters received and letters written under each daily entry. She would buy wads of stamps at the Post Office, and we were constantly being asked 'to run to the letter box' to mail her letters. The result was that she received letters from every corner all her life, and some she stored safely.

Daphne also kept up correspondence with relatives around the world. It was natural, when she and Don spent a year in the States, that they would meet up with some of them, who were about the same age as Daphne. These were the grandchildren and great grandchildren of emigrants from Meath. Their grandparents and Daphne's Grannie had been brothers and sisters. Great discussions took place as to how to introduce the next generation to each other. The idea of a Family Reunion developed, and was kept brewing by Daphne's letter writing after she had returned to Dublin. Daphne's sister Dorothy and her husband offered to organise a Reunion for 1983, based in Ontario. Close to a hundred attended from around the world, and a repeat was promised in five years' time. Since then, Family Reunions have been held every five years, located successively in Boston, Sioux City, Athlone, Whistler, New York and Stratford-upon-Avon. The generations have come together well. Daphne's contributions included organisation, booklet writing and the development of an ecumenical church service, at which she would preach a carefully prepared sermon. Her chief concern was inclusiveness, that all should feel welcome. Those married to family, 'the Outlaws', were to receive a warm welcome and to be involved at all levels.

Despite all of these activities Daphne joyfully seized many opportunities for foreign travel with family or friends. She visited Denmark, France, Germany, Greece, Italy, India, Galapagos Islands, Finland, Czechoslovakia, Australia and the Arctic Ocean. It was the people, their history, monuments and art that fascinated her.

Leslie Greer (*née* Tyrrell), a good friend, wrote after Daphne's death, 'Even after her most important work had been accomplished, 'retirement' was not a word in Daphne's vocabulary. As she demonstrated in her eighties, being active in Rathmichael Parish as a Lay Reader to within three weeks of her death, and as one of the Meals on Wheels team driving around, bringing food and a smile to people who were usually some years younger than herself.

'Her social life was cheerfully filled with visits to the theatre, membership of the poetry-reading group, attendance at a Synge Summer School, short holidays with friends in Ireland, friendship with an Angolan family seeking asylum in Ireland and, perhaps most Daphne-like, keeping in touch with people who might be lonely. Remarkably she once said she was never bored. How many could say the like? She never used a walking stick. Shankill, where she lived for many years, seems empty without her.'

When Daphne first came to Ireland, a favourite activity for her was to accompany her Uncle Charlie Murphy and his wife, Amos, on excursions to every part of the country. Charlie was Secretary of the Automobile Association, and he was Architect for the Church of Ireland. His duties required that he visit and inspect churches, rectories and other church buildings from one end of the island to the other. At the same time he would examine and grade hotels for the Automobile Association. Few Irishmen were privileged to know Ireland in the way he did. And there was another group he liked to check up on. He would say, 'Never forget the poor widows of Anglo-Ireland.' Isolated in big houses on large estates, many of them couldn't cope. Frequently, the houses would be falling into disrepair, the farmland would be poorly managed. Charlie knew most Protestants in Ireland, and their personal situations. With whomever of his own family he had in tow, he would sweep up the driveways where few cars had gone before, and bring some good cheer and some worldly news. These experiences in the 1930s had a profound effect on a nineteen-year-old prairie girl, his niece Daphne. She never forgot the lonely, even when she herself, in her eighties, felt isolated from three of her four children, all of her grandchildren, and was solitary without her Donald.

As the 1990s progressed, Daphne gradually made decisions to withdraw from various committees on which she sat. The over-riding issues were the driving into town, as the traffic conditions deteriorated, or the walking from the Dart Station to her destination. The few activities she managed to maintain were made possible by the great care and consideration given by others to her and to her friend Leslie Greer, most particularly by Melissa Webb (née Stanford) providing assistance up and down steps, and along broken up pathways. I asked Daphne how these noble caregivers could be properly thanked, and she said, 'Do the same to other old people as you go through life.'

In April 1999, she sent in her resignation to the Committee of the Trinity College Dublin Association and Trust. She received a reply from Chairman

Peter Ledbetter, which in part states:

> Your commitment to the Association and Trust over many years has been most valuable and many of the Committee expressed their appreciation for all you have done. I write on their behalf, and my own, to thank you for your contribution to and your keen interest in the activities of the Association and Trust.

While living on Sandyford Road, Daphne assisted in some Taney Parish services, with the Rector, Canon Walter Burrows. When Daphne and Don moved from Gatineau to Seaview Park in Shankill, in 1982, Rector Billy Marshall, and later Rector Fred Appelbe, welcomed her participation as a Lay Reader in Rathmichael parish. She was delighted to contribute in any way she could, occasionally preaching, frequently assisting during Sunday services and at the altar during Holy Communion. She participated in the weekly early Morning Prayer services for Peace, and she conducted quiet services in a local nursing home every Wednesday for many years.

Not many knew how meaningful it was for her to sit in the chair near the altar of Rathmichael Church, under the brass plaque placed there by parishioners on the death of a former rector. The plaque states:

TO THE BEAUTIFYING OF THIS CHURCH

AND IN AFFECTIONATE MEMORY OF

JOHN JEFFCOTT DILLON, B.D.

RECTOR OF RATHMICHAEL 1890–1912 DIED GOOD FRIDAY 1912.

THESE PRAYER DESKS AND SEATS, THE MOSAICS ON THE

CHANCEL WALL, THE MARBLE SLAB BENEATH THE HOLY TABLE

HAVE BEEN PRESENTED BY PARISHIONERS AND OTHER FRIENDS.

"Remember them who have spoken unto you the word

of God: whose faith follow"   HEBREWS XIII.7.

John Jeffcott Dillon was the brother of Daphne's grandmother, her father's mother, Anna Maria (Dillon) Wallace. John had married Nellie Snow. Becoming a minister in the Church of Ireland, his last parish had been Rathmichael. Together, John and Nellie had ministered out of Rathmichael Rectory. Nellie died prematurely, and John had, in his grief, developed nooks and crannies, with benches, in the grounds of the country Rectory. Here he would sit peacefully, remembering his Nellie, and writing in his diary. Daphne's middle name was Dillon, and she was so named after her grandmother's family. She felt a circle had been completed when she sat under the Dillon plaque as a Lay Reader.

17

WOMEN'S MINISTRY IN THE CHURCH OF IRELAND

Daphne's name is well known as one of the principal pioneers for the ordination of women in the Church of Ireland. She was one of the first woman Lay Readers commissioned in 1975.

By the early 1970s, Daphne was known by those in the Church of Ireland as an academic participant, who wrote balanced articles on a number of topics of interest to clergy and laity alike. Daphne said, 'George Simms, who was by now Archbishop of Armagh and Primate of All Ireland, had a publication going, and he asked me to write an article about 'Women in the Church.' I sat down one day when I had a quiet hour and I began to think of some people who might be interested, some women I knew. And it suddenly came to me that not one of them would go into a job in the Church unless they could be ordained. No use being a second-class citizen. They wouldn't be interested. If they were going to give their life to this job, they would have to be allowed to do it fully. I stood up, and I never changed my mind. The nearest thing I had to a revelation. I never changed my mind one half minute after that.'

'Women and the Church'[9] was published by 'New Divinity – a Church of Ireland Journal', in the November 1970 issue, Volume 1, No. 2. In this, one of her strongest statements about women's involvement, Daphne forcefully

[9] The full text of the essay is given in Appendix 1

made her point to the Church of Ireland community. There was no need to spell it out again. It was now known how she felt.

The final paragraph reads:

I believe the Church is facing another crisis of direction at the moment. I see its urgent immediate task to be the fostering of Christian community. All of us, men and women, need to gather together in a depth not reached in most parish worship so that we may scatter as more effective Christians. This should be familiar ground for the church: the building of Koinonia 'where there is neither Jew nor Greek, male nor female.' But you cannot proclaim community and practise exclusiveness. What is needed is the same spirit which inspired the actions of the second-class Jewish citizen when he allowed himself to be drawn into public discussion at the well with someone who was not only a Samaritan, but also a woman. Women much appreciate the help of those who are following in his footsteps and taking up our cause with vision and courage. There are indeed signs that the countryside is opening up before us; perhaps along one of the new highways, bishops may yet be bringing their husbands to Lambeth.

Daphne said, 'It was curious how everything fell into place. I was teaching History of Art at the High School every Friday morning. It had become more and more unsatisfactory, as they didn't have any equipment, and I used to have to bring it in from home. Eventually, early one Friday I woke up, and said to Donald, 'I've done this long enough. It's not very satisfactory.' Don replied, 'Well, you'd better tell the headmaster.' So I did, and the headmaster understood.

'Strangely, on the following Monday morning I received a letter from Archbishop Buchanan asking me to be a Lay Reader. Just like that. What a coincidence! He said he would be offering a training course himself, a course in Theology. The goal was to increase the participation of women in the life of the Church. It was a renewal of a similar request made earlier, which had not materialised successfully. This time, there would be a total of five women who would train together.'

The Archbishop had asked the Diocesan Synods 'Is it right to limit the possibility of ordination to one half of the Church? Our House of Bishops has recently echoed the view of Lambeth that there is no theological reason against the ordination of women. The Church in Canada has already decided in favour... the Church of Ireland should at least declare its mind on the subject.'

In June, 1975, Daphne delivered a 'small talk' on 'Religious Education of the Child' to a seminar of teachers and clergy in Tralee, organized by Revd William Pike, Rector of Tralee. It wasn't long before Daphne was giving an address in Christ Church Cathedral in Waterford, as follows:

'Thank you, Mr Dean, for your introduction, which was very kind, and for your invitation to speak here tonight, which I accept as an honour paid to women in general by the Church.

We need all the encouragement we can get from men and women, as this rôle is very new to us. It is so new that we do not even know how we should dress for it. A man speaking in church wears no hat and a white collar; it is only a question of which way the collar is turned. But with us, it is not so straightforward. I looked at a little black hat that I have, and then remembered that the last time I spoke in church I had worn that hat, and my husband had said, as I left the house, 'So you have your biretta on to-night. Are you going to hear confessions?' Well, it has not come to that, and I don't want it to.

I was thinking as I drove down, here I am in 1974 at the same stage of my life as was my grandmother in 1900. What a century of change it has been, with our cars and domestic gadgets, TV and radio communication, telephones and flying the Atlantic. But none of these inventions mark my life off from my grandmother's, as does the emancipation of women. What really makes the difference between her life and mine is that, in spite of having a husband and four children, from within my own home I am able to have a life of my own, make my own contacts, do my own thing. And almost as remarkable, when I think of my grandfathers, is that in all this I have the encouragement and active co-operation of my husband. In spite of subterranean grumblings, women continue to expand their activities, but not much in the Church. Only *there* is there very little new opening, a sort of stalemate instead of an expansion.

Have you ever thought where do women *not* work, side by side, on equal terms with men? The armed forces, monasteries – even the stock exchange, all have now opened their doors. But not the Church.

I am very privileged to be speaking here during your renewal week. My theme tonight is that the Church is facing a crisis, and while we have faith that the new life will emerge, it cannot be achieved without a full contribution from both men and women. 'He that will not apply new

159

remedies must expect new evils,' said Francis Bacon. I see very clearly that the Church needs all the help from women that we are prepared to give. For centuries we have done much for the physical beauty of the Church and for the comfort of its members. Long may this continue. But when, apart from nunneries, have we been involved spiritually, have we been consulted about vital church matters, have we been in on important policy decisions? I suggest that the practice should be to ask women what they would like to do for the Church, and, then, that they should be given the opportunity to do it. I suggest that clergy delegate some real responsibility to us, and that the Church provide fit training and preparation for that responsibility. And which responsibilities? There will be different answers from different women, and here is the crunch. If a woman believes she has a vocation to be ordained, she should, in my opinion, be listened to as if she were a man. She should be allowed to be ordained, if she is considered suitable, as a man would be.

In one of her weekly letters to me, in Canada, dated 28th September, 1975, Daphne wrote:

Tomorrow evening those of us who are to be commissioned as Lay Readers in Christ Church Cathedral on 16th November are meeting to make some kind of a decision about what we shall *wear*. Not easy but the Archbishop has left it to us; the only thing he suggested we try to look as pretty and feminine as possible. So far, the unanimous choice seems to be for a long pale luminous grey pinafore with bright green silk blouse. Three of us would like to go further and use the liturgical colours for a blouse change during the seasons of the Christian year. And if you are wondering what the liturgical colours are, you know no more than I did until ten days ago. Roughly, they are violet for Lent, white for Whitsuntide, possibly yellow for Easter and green for all the Sundays between Trinity Sunday and Advent (green being the colour for growth). At least, by deciding on green we are in keeping with the present season, and I have hopes that we might gradually introduce the other colours. So many of my friends are repelled by the dreariness of the Church of Ireland ... and what a visual aid for children it would be if you could use your clothes as an introduction. The opposition comes from those who would think we were setting ourselves up by being gimmicky and so we might antagonise the person in the pew. *Oh Dear!* At least we don't have to look like half-frocked curates with things hung around our necks, and big awkward sleeves that would get caught in the eagle's wings!

On 20th October, 1975, she wrote:

Trying to get ready for our commissioning, our recent concern has been – of all things – with what we are to wear. We took the decision too lightly, not allowing for the difficulties which would arise. At first we were given an entirely free choice ... so with much discussion the consensus was for the grey pinafore with a deep apple green blouse. Not acceptable to the establishment. So we chose a cherry red long gown with fluted skirt. Then we were told it was too bright and that it might be best for our authority if we had a preaching scarf which had to be blue (Lay Readers' colour.) Mrs Buchanan, the Archbishop's wife, was in the choosing by this time, and we were under the impression for several days that we would be clothed in *grey* with this dull blue thing hung round our necks, and we were all very upset and dispirited (phone calls galore, no swearing but near to it.) However, when we went to the Archbishop's house for the absolutely final decision last Thursday, Mrs B. had a lovely magenta shade for our gown (we all liked the style) and she had had the bright idea of a pale blue (in fact, St Patrick's blue) preaching scarf, each one to be made individually and put on us in the cathedral at the time of the commissioning. I'm to go tomorrow for my fitting for a strange garment. I hope everything will be all right. We also are thinking of exams in Ecclesiastical History, Old and New Testament, too; the men Lay Readers do an exam and the Arch does not want us to appear to be less well trained. He is setting the papers, marking them and also, I believe, going to tell us what will be on them! He has no great reverence for exams, and apparently is very impressed with our dedication and interest, so I gather we have passed already. But, as I say to Don, I don't want to make it too embarrassing for the poor man, though I must admit I find it very hard to learn anything *off* at the moment. But lay reading is not really about these things. I am afraid that lately my thoughts have lacked focus. Let's hope I can get a little quieter and more withdrawn in the next few weeks.

There was a postal strike in Canada from the end of October through to early December, 1975, so the next letter was not written until 7th December, 1975:

The big event for me this autumn has, of course, been my commissioning;

it took place as scheduled on 16th November in Christ Church Cathedral. Both the Archbishop and the Dean went to immense trouble to plan a meaningful service and to take it with sincerity and enthusiasm. The cathedral was nearly full which gave us much needed support and encouragement. Many of our friends kindly turned up, even Betty Cole (*née* Harman) from Cavan ('for your ordination' she wrote). She came to stay here for three days afterwards and we had some good chats.

Possibly, when I last wrote we were having intense consultation over the garment we were to be decked in; miraculously, that's the word when you consider the difficulties we got into over it, but anyway it was all harmoniously resolved in the end. We chose a long fitted gown of deep magenta with a mandarin collar and for the badge of our office we had a preaching scarf/stole of St Patrick's pale blue. Really very effective. It was the Archbishop who finally suggested the deep red. He said, 'If they like to think I am commissioning five lady bishops, let them think it!' His text for his sermon was 'I have chosen you, you have not chosen me.' After the ceremony we were asked, as a congregation of about 300, down to the crypt for tea; a substantial one with really good sandwiches and cakes.

The very next Sunday after the commissioning the Archbishop had arranged to come to our home parish, Taney, for his annual visit and the Rector, Canon Walter Burrows, asked Patricia Hastings-Hardy, another Lay Reader, and me to give a little help with the service. My job was to read the epistle. I have done this before so that was no great step forward. But it was satisfactory to robe and sit up in the stall with the choir, in the place where the curate, Horace McKinley, usually sits. You feel so much more involved if you are where the action is; it is an altogether different sensation. Since then I have had no duties but I have been asked to preach in College Chapel on St Brigid's Day (1st February) and in Stillorgan on March 28th (Mothering Sunday.) I asked the question 'When is Fathering Sunday?' and got no answer. I have also been asked to do an Outlook (3½ minute talk on Radio Telefís Éireann late each night) at the end of March. The producer for the program wrote congratulating me 'on taking the silk.' I replied that I 'had taken the cotton.'

That will be enough preaching for the present. I shall refuse anything further, but I would be ready to read the service, if asked. Preaching is just one huge nightmare. It fills me with solid terror.

At the Mothering Sunday address in Stillorgan mentioned above, Daphne began:

> I should like to thank your Rector most warmly for inviting me to speak here in the very early days of my Lay Readership. I was asked the other day how I felt to be spreading my wings, and I could only reply that we were recently hatched out and had not yet got our pin feathers, so it might be better to walk before we took off in flight. But I do not need to have even a flight of fantasy to know that this is called Mothering Sunday. Hearing the official title brought me down to earth very quickly and I took a step or two backwards with a jerk, for the ordinary reason that I would much rather see it called Parenting Sunday. The church does not recognise Father's Day, and I hope they do not start to do so, because is it not better to think of both parents together, having the care and responsibility for their children? There is much talk about Women's Lib, but what about Men's Lib, in this matter at any rate? I am a bit weary of the assumption that men are only second-class parents. At the same time, I must say that this situation has much improved since our eldest was a child in his pram when my husband took him for a walk along the streets, not a hundred miles from here. He was followed by about thirty children, who crept closer and closer, making remarks like, 'Poor man, his wife must be dead.' This drove my husband back to take cover behind as many doors as possible. That, I think, would not happen to-day.

Not long afterwards she wrote:

> Last week I helped a man Lay Reader take Morning Prayer, the first time I had read the service without preaching. Most people were very kind as we shook hands at the door afterwards, but I did notice one middle-aged woman, who refused to even look at me. The male Lay Reader whom I was helping rang me up later and said that my presence had been well received by the majority of the congregation. Sometime I might get up courage to ask what the minority had said. Middle-aged women can be quite horrified by the prospect of a woman Lay Reader.

As time went by, Daphne learned that the preparation of her sermons would require ten hours for every minute that she spoke. She practised by reading into a tape recorder, and to family members. She constantly critiqued her writings and her delivery. 'Sermon too long. I lack warmth. What to do?' On another occasion, '30 people came to the service, scattered about in a church that could hold 200. I felt I didn't go down very well. Scarcely a remark made to me afterwards, except "that must have been an ordeal"!' Daphne took some courses on communication, and soon found that preaching came more easily than before. Many parishes welcomed her with open arms. I accompanied her several times. I remember once when, after driving for several hours, we were met 'at the crossroads at 9:00' by a parishioner. We were led to his home, where we could freshen up. Daphne wrote: 'Gave us coffee in the kitchen and we talked of beekeeping, and winemaking from sloes, blackberries and elder flowers.' After preaching in two different churches, we were escorted to another local home for a most delicious country Sunday dinner. I can still taste the gooseberry fool! We talked of that day years afterwards.

As part of a Lenten Sunday Morning series offered in St Bartholomew's, Clyde Road, in 1977, Daphne, listed as being 'Adult Education Council Member and Lay Reader' gave a talk on 'Communicating the Faith by adult education.' She was combining her experiences into one. John Paterson was the Vicar. A talk on the previous Sunday was given by Horace McKinley, by now Rector at Whitechurch. He had become a family friend while a curate at Taney.

Horace McKinley wrote in his 'Appreciation' published in *The Irish Times* after Daphne died, 'Daphne did not consider herself a feminist, choosing instead to think of men and women as different yet complementary, but also equal in the sight of God... Her own personal support was of unstinting encouragement to those women who felt they had a vocation waiting to be tested by the Church.'

In 1979, a booklet titled 'Should we have women priests?' was published by the APCK. Reverend Dr Michael Kennedy is today a widely recognised scholar of the Church of Ireland, is Rector of Lisnadill and Kildarton in the Armagh Diocese, and is a Canon of St Patrick's Cathedral in Dublin. He has described the development of this booklet, copies of which were sent to every diocesan synodsman or synodswoman in the whole Church of Ireland, as the matter was being referred for discussion to the Diocesan Synods:

I was giving a paper on an unrelated subject to the Belfast Clerical Union, and after the session the Very Rev'd (later Bishop) Gilbert Wilson came up to me and asked, 'I understand you are in favour of Women's Ordination?' I said, 'Yes,' and girded myself for battle! However, wearing his hat as the big wheel in the APCK he said they were thinking of publishing 5,000 word essays for and against on this issue. Would I be interested and would I share this work with someone else? Of course I agreed, and was put in touch with Daphne.

My recollection is that I did an initial draft and we went through it critically. I remember Daphne persuading me to sharpen some of the material on the first page! Daphne meanwhile had got in touch with various people in the U.S. and we were able to incorporate their material into our essay.

Our methodology was to try to anticipate what opponents would say and to counter it. In the event I think we stated their case much better than they did with their counter-arguments. Their essay was in two unreconciled pieces. Our essay was very much a 'first effort' and the debate became more sophisticated as the years went on. But I still think we did a good job and helped to move things forward.

I wish we had known then of the evidence for women priests (and even bishops!) within early Christianity.

With Daphne's guidance a group of women from various churches, calling themselves St Brigid's Society, had got together for mutual encouragement and for discussions on the issues of women's ministry and ordination.

Daphne said, 'Frank Luce had had a movement for the Ordination of Women for ten years, but he had been voted down, defeated in a General Synod vote. Frank really led the way, but you can't go on when you have been defeated.' The straw vote in the Diocesan Synods had gone in favour, but the General Synod failed to achieve the necessary majority in the House of Clergy by a small margin.

The opening of the diaconate was made possible by the passing of a Bill for Women's Ordination as Deacons (to the Diaconate). A Deacon is a sort of Apprentice Priest in the Anglican Communion. Normally, you have to serve a year as a Deacon before you can be 'priested': but once you are a Deacon you are defined as 'Clergy' and you are expected to wear a 'dog collar' when on duty.

After the Church of Ireland finally approved women's ordination to the diaconate in 1984, this gave way to a specific Church of Ireland group, the Women's Ministry Group, which studied the issues and strategies required to encourage both the vocations and the acceptance of women leading worship.

This was the only organization in the Church of Ireland actively promoting the cause. The official birth of the Women's Ministry Group in the Church of Ireland late in 1986 was accomplished with the support of the House of Bishops.

Daphne was the obvious person to take the chair of the Women's Ministry Group, with Michael Kennedy as Vice-Chair. Daphne impressed on the committee that the public image of the Women's Ministry Group must be neither strident nor pushy. In the organisation of any public meetings or debates, Daphne ensured that invitations were issued to a wide audience both of supporters and objectors as the views of everybody needed voice. Daphne researched widely on the successes and conflicts of women in ministry around the world through publications and in active correspondence with women abroad. She shared experiences and learned of regional difficulties from friends and acquaintances in places as far flung as all parts of the UK, Vancouver, Chicago and Australia. Long before e-mails, women heard of Daphne and wrote to her out of the blue. She had great interest in what she was told, and always wrote back personal letters, sharing information and requesting further details. This useful knowledge was shared with the committee and was very helpful as on the one hand it inspired hope, but also gave examples of how not to proceed.

The group arranged study evenings in Trinity in the winter of 1985–86, to look closely at the biblical material and the experiences of other churches that had ordained women.

Daphne said, 'Diana McClatchey used to live in Dublin. Her husband had been the first Appointments Officer in Trinity, and through that connection I knew her quite well. We had kept in touch. She had become the Vice Moderator of the Movement for the Ordination of Women in England.'

The Archbishop of Canterbury, Robert Runcie, had been advocating 'gradualism,' emphasising that women needed more experience as ordained deacons or lay ministers before any change was made. Diana McClatchey, now a Deaconess, stood firm. She said, 'I wonder if you are really aware that there is a struggle afoot to make it possible for a generation of young women to find a place for themselves in the Christian tradition.' She argued that these women would be driven into underground churches meeting in homes or completely out of the faith, if the church 'retains the atmosphere of an exclusive men's club on ladies' night.'

Daphne continued, 'Diana wrote saying we should be doing something about ordination of women in Ireland. We asked her over to Dublin on several occasions, and she stayed with us. I invited Ginnie Kennerley, who was a professional journalist, to come out and interview Diana. The article was published, which kept our movement to the fore.

'We kept in touch with Ginnie Kennerley, who was becoming interested and soon became a constant member of the group. Between us we decided we should have a conference on Women's Ministry in the Church of Ireland, to let some people talk and listen. It took a whole year to organise. Some men were on the organising panel, and the Conference on Women's Ministry spread across a whole day. It was held on 11ᵗʰ April 1986 in Trinity, in one of the theatres in the New Arts Block. About one hundred people came, some from the North, some from the country, but mostly from Dublin. It went well. Our aim was not to be confrontational, but rather how to be inclusive. Many Church of Ireland clergy attended, men who knew well the needs of their parishes, needs that would be met only by giving women greater stature. Diana McClatchey presented a paper on "The Role of the Woman Deacon in the Church".'

Daphne herself addressed the Women's Conference in College Chapel. This was her address:

Women's Ministry
April, 1986

In the name of God, Father, Son and Holy Spirit

I begin my address with words of thanks to the Reverend Kenneth Kearon who most hospitably put his chapel at our disposal for the opening of our conference on women's ministry. I trust that Queen Elizabeth the First, the foundress of this College, would have approved of this action — and of ours.

It is, I hope, auspicious that this conference is being held during the Easter season. Like all Christians, women think of themselves as Easter people. We lift our eyes from the lesser concerns of life to the glorious message of Easter, and know that 'all manner of things shall be well.' Easter speaks to us of renewal, of the releasing of more abundant life, of amazing victory where before there was despair, and of the triumph of love over the dark powers of evil.

Why do we, as women, at this time see ourselves as having a vocation to express this in ministry in the Church? For one thing, women in the western world have been set free from much ill-health, and also from the worst shackles of domestic chores. We are now as well educated as men. Those of us who have children have families of manageable size; those who do not are as free as any man. Many of us, therefore, could be *available* in new ways to devote untapped resources of energy, talent, and time to the service of the Church. In what capacity?

We have a long and wide experience of nurturing at all levels, whether at home, or in the many caring professions which have been opened to women in the last hundred years. We have a facility for gathering people together to promote a sense of community and wholeness. Generally, we like to gather and *include*, not *exclude* others. Nor is it always recognised how practised we are in making decisions, many of which may even affect life and death. Nurturing, the promotion of community and wholeness, and a familiarity with decision-making — these qualities, with others, could present the Church with a wealth of talented skills which it can ill-afford to ignore. Our contribution to the decorating of churches, of even the making of tea, should never be underestimated, but it must not stop there. We can also serve with real responsibility in areas such as pastoral care in parishes, leading prayer and study groups, liturgical ministry, the healing of the sick. Our place is, indeed, in the home, because *the world is our home*.

What we are asking to-day of this conference is that it should focus on making the Easter message come alive for women and the church, so that our talents and our new availability can be channelled into the service of the Christian community. I take this opportunity of paying tribute to the thousands of lay women who already enrich our parishes, with their quiet and dedicated ministry. We are not unconcerned with the setting out of structures for women's roles, but we are also talking about renewal. We look for signs of organic growth, as a bulb develops into a flower, or a small seed becomes a strong tree. And, for this prophetic mission, we invoke the power of the Holy Spirit.

This leads on naturally to mention of the diaconate, an historic order now open to women in the Church of Ireland. How are we to develop its potential? Jesus Christ established a new covenant, in which service to God is encompassed in serving one's fellows. In this, the early deacons were in the forefront, many women among them. 'Receive her in the name of the Lord,' wrote St Paul, of Phoebe.

We pray for inspiration as we seek 'not to destroy tradition, but to try to

discover a fuller, richer truth cradled in what the church has safeguarded.'
May our vision come true! Amen.

Of the period following the Conference, Daphne said: 'Horace McKinley, now
Rector over in Whitechurch, was very involved. He kept saying, 'Remember,
when this is over, don't let it slip. You've gone a certain distance, and keep going
if you can.'

In a later comment, recorded on tape, Daphne said:

> There was opposition to the Ordination of Women right from the first. A
> group of people objecting to the idea, most of them 'concerned clergy,' got
> together and sent out leaflets to people who had been at the Conference. But
> that didn't work very well. People were not impressed. It did more harm to
> their cause than good, for people didn't think they should be told what to
> do.
>
> We followed Horace's advice; and we held a meeting in this house. This
> was followed by many more meetings held here, at 44 Seaview Park. Donald
> was behind us. He answered the door, took people's coats, and sometimes
> gave us wine to keep us going. He would sit quietly over by the fireside,
> reading and listening.
>
> When Ginnie began to discover that she might have a vocation, the
> movement was given quite a push forward. It all began happening very much
> at one time. There were several people who had been ordained in other
> churches, some Presbyterians, that we invited out to our meetings. In fact,
> all kinds of people came and went. Some felt we were too staid, they wanted
> us to be more emotional. But it wasn't our way of going about it. We just kept
> going forward, we kept on making progress.

Towards the middle of April, 1986, Daphne and Don went on a cathedral tour
in England, to hear Easter music, with Daphne's sister Dorothy and her
husband. They visited eight cathedrals, staying with relatives along the way.
The tour was to include a Ministry of Women Conference to be held in
Canterbury, where Daphne met up with Patricia Hastings-Hardy. Much of the
Conference took place in Canterbury Cathedral, and Daphne referred to it in
letters as her 'Canterbury Pilgrimage.' She wrote in her diary:

> Went to rehearsal in Cathedral, robed among much query and apparent
> admiration of our gowns, walked in sunshine and joined a long, impressive
> procession in the precincts. At precisely noon (this is England) we moved in

through the west door. Seating arrangements awry, but the Cathedral reverberated with a thousand voices, sparkled with a thousand candles. I watched carefully for my cue. Just after Mary Tanner preached on 'Wholeness' I then read the words in Irish and English, 'I bring you peace from the Church in Ireland.' Received Holy Communion from a Puerto Rican priest who looked one straight in the eye with joy. When service over and bishops had left, when women started to process out, there was a sudden explosion of clapping. I thought it was hailstones falling, at first! It kept on and on until the last woman had processed out – their dear hands must have been very sore. Found Don who immediately kissed me with tears in his eyes.

In a letter written after the conference, Donald noted, 'I was very proud of D when she stood up before a congregation of a thousand in Canterbury Cathedral and gave greetings of peace from Ireland.' Daphne composed a list of the contacts she made at this conference, the people and their homelands: 'Kenya, Black USA, lay Native Indian from Alert Bay in Canada, Melbourne in Australia, Hong Kong and Toronto.'

Patricia Hastings-Hardy recounted that when she and Daphne processed together, Daphne's thoughts, always, were that they should have a quiet, dignified presence. When asked about this, Daphne replied simply, 'Dignity and Grace.' It was in contrast with parts of the women's liberation movement that were showing a strident edge. In the Church of England, the Movement for Women's Ordination was now experiencing some difficulties. The early women Lay Readers in the Church of Ireland felt that they would be most effective by bearing themselves calmly with dignity and grace.

Daphne was frequently being invited to preach. Clergy discovered that she would be willing to travel far and wide to participate with them in church services, or to hold the fort for them while they took some time out. She delivered sermons from Tullow and Cork to Armagh, from Westport to Stradbally, to Navan and all around Dublin, both city and county. This might not have always been easy. How many times was the lectern on the pulpit too high for her to reach? Or the steps up to the pulpit too steep for someone in their seventies, who was five feet one inch tall, and who was wearing a full-length robe? At one service she had left her reading glasses at home, at another service she muddled collects, gospels and prayers. Once she wrote: 'Forgot the psalm and forgot to go to the door.' But her demeanour was such that these troubles did not intrude.

On June 30, 1987 Daphne was in Glenstal, Limerick, addressing the Ecumenical Conference. She said, in part:

My godmother told me that during my baptism she looked down over the white bundle in her arms and noticed that my father was wearing boots which did not match. I have sometimes thought since, that those odd boots are symbolic of my attitude to the institutional church.

For many years, I occupied a boundary position, half-believer, half-agnostic, though mine was always an Anglican agnosticism. I eventually found a little piece of rock to stand on. This was largely due to the influence of a few, dedicated people in the Anglican Communion, most of whom were ordained. When, subsequently, the late Archbishop of Dublin, Dr Buchanan, asked me to be commissioned as a Lay Reader, I found myself accepting, though with some trepidation.

As most of you will be aware, a reader in the Church of Ireland is normally commissioned to read the full service of matins and evensong (save only the absolution), and in the new Eucharistic rite, may read the Gospel and pass the chalice. I was very honoured to be numbered among the first five Anglican women to be commissioned in Dublin. I would like to pay tribute to all those who have made us feel welcome and needed. I am personally, deeply grateful to clergy, church members and congregations who have given me support and appreciation. It is also most humbling to frequently find respect for my commitment from those outside the church.

My ministry has deepened my own spiritual life, in part because it has thrown me into closer contact with the quiet church, made up of unassuming, practising Christians. Probably but for my ministry, I would never have met most of them, let alone discussed religion with them. I now also have a more informed awareness of some of the difficulties which those who are ordained must face – how testing it is to write a sermon, how draining physically and emotionally to take a church service. And I have come to understand how isolated the clergy, their wives, and indeed their families can often feel. I even begin to comprehend, though with difficulty, how some clergy feel threatened by new ideas and new people from without; for example, by women. We laity are also under threat – sometimes not allowed to forget our proper station. A dear old lady greeted me warmly at the door of a church where I had conducted the full service. As she shook my hand she said, 'A lovely day, dear, but you'd miss the Rector terribly, wouldn't you?'

In the twelve years since I was commissioned there has been a steady growth in lay ministry throughout the Church, corresponding to a changing attitude in society. Everywhere there is a shift from emphasis on the individual to the idea of community and co-operation. Worker participation in industry, resident associations, PTAs, even support groups like AA, all point in the same direction. The Church is beginning to accept the statement, quoted in the report of the Church of Ireland commission on the ministry, of which I was a member. 'The rôle of the laity is what the Church is all about – all else is subordinate.' Christ's lay ministry predates all those further rôles of prophet and priest, which have been attributed to him over the years. Moreover, the ordained ministry is by now realising the great importance of their rôle in enabling lay people to fulfil their ministry. With the best will in the world, such sharing is sometimes difficult, but I have noticed that openness, flexibility and mutual trust lead to a way being found. I like the suggestion that a start is best made when groups of committed Christians come together to talk informally about how they are trying to live out their Christianity. ... I'd like to see the church showing a new vision of its mission. Let us stop being so preoccupied with moral questions, important though they are, and let us try to emphasise the Christian message of peace and joy. Let us be able to account for the belief that in Christ's death and resurrection, evil has been faced and conquered, and that this has nothing to do with worldly success. Instead, this is an acknowledgement of our dependence on the providence and love of God, from which nothing can separate us. This proclamation is our hope and our joy, and needs to be taken out into the marketplace, and into our homes, in language which can be understood by ordinary people. Let me express the hope that in Glenstal we shall not be talking to ourselves, but that clergy and laity, in partnership, may be learning how to handle the situation. The Lambeth report of 1978 said that the laity go where the clergy do not go, and speak where the clergy are not heard. Most of us have first-hand knowledge of the spiritual void in the world about us. Do the clergy have that knowledge, too? We look for the strength that comes from worship under the leadership of the clergy, who are also uniquely situated to give us spiritual guidance. We ask that you lend us a listening ear, and entrust us with more responsibility.

It was St Augustine who said, 'When I am frightened by what I am to you, I am consoled by what I am with you. *To* you, I am a bishop: *with* you

I am a Christian. What I am to you is an office and a danger; what I am with you is grace and salvation.'

In the Spring of 1988, Daphne wrote: 'There was a very large and successful Women's Ecumenical Gathering in Kildare Cathedral. The Cathedral was full, and everyone from north, south, east and west was so happy.'

Ginnie Kennerley wrote: '1988 was the year I was ordained Deacon. The process for women's ordination to the priesthood took two years, starting with approval of the bill going forward the following year in 1989, so there was also great excitement that year when the House voted to allow the Bill to go forward for a vote to be held in 1990.'

It was about this time that I received a tea towel as a gift from Daphne. It was purple linen, with white lettering which said: 'A woman's place is in the House of Bishops.' It hung proudly on our kitchen wall, and caused many exciting conversations for all the young mothers who used to gather regularly at the kitchen table for tea.

On 14th March, 1989, Daphne wrote: 'Did I tell you I was preaching in Christ Church Cathedral in Dublin recently? I believe I was the first woman to ever do so. It was to Guiders on the occasion of the 100th anniversary of the birth of Lady Baden-Powell. There were some men there, too! I walked up the aisle beside John Paterson. It was his first Sunday as Dean. Give him his due, he is always friendly – some of the other opponents, and indeed some on the fence, just run when they see me!'

In May, 1989, Daphne was preaching one Sunday evening on 'Meditation for Women's Fellowship'. She concluded as follows:

As Christian women in what looks like being a new age, I believe we have a special role to play in this joyful open-mindedness of which I have been speaking. We have a God-given duty to contribute feminine experience and imagination for the benefit of our society. There is good precedent in the scriptures, where the rôle of many women may be understated. But it is there for the searching, if we look for it, with the renewed vision which we have just been singing about in our evensong.

Daphne said, 'In 1988–1990, the Archbishop of Dublin offered a two-year course in theology. The aim of the course was to provide a programme of study, leading to a deeper understanding of the Christian Faith. Anyone from the United Diocese who wished to undertake a concentrated course of study was welcomed. Readers, Sunday School Teachers, Study Group Leaders and Church Officers benefited from this course.'

A Select Committee on Women's Ministry was set up which produced a very fine report in 1989.

Daphne said, 'In 1990, the General Synod of the Church of Ireland, which is part lay and part clerical, met to discuss and vote on ordination of women. It was held in the Royal Dublin Society. I went in for a couple of days during the early discussions. We were not a part of the Synod, so we members of the Committee of the Women's Ministry Group sat at the back. I remember Hazel Tamplin came in and said, 'In the name of sanity, when are they going to pass this? It should be obvious. I've never heard such nonsense.'

'We all sat there at the back. And the man behind me said, 'You should be minding your own business in England.' I think he mistook me for Diana McClatchey, so I turned around and said, 'What are you talking about? I'm a Reader in the Church of Ireland.' He blushed.

'The day of the final vote, I couldn't go in. I just couldn't face it. Everyone on the Synod has a vote in a case like this. There was a YES door and a NO door, and, apparently on this occasion, a big crowd went to the YES door. Some in the back thought people were making a mistake, that they had gone to the wrong door in a muddle. But by this stage the majority was supportive. My brother-in-law, visiting from Canada, had gone in to watch and to give me the result. He shot to the phone, and called before even the press had the news! It went through just a month before Donald died.

'I was always very careful about discussing the ordination issue. Many people were more or less in favour, but not quite. I've noticed about Ireland that it is a very conservative country, but if a thing begins to go forward, it does so in leaps. It was very satisfactory that it went through. Then, Ginnie Kennerley became the first woman to be ordained in Dublin. A number of Catholics attended her service.'

Ginnie Kennerley wrote: 'So the Bill was passed by the required two thirds majorities, of the houses of the clergy and, separately, of the laity, and by a majority believed to be 9 – 3 in the House of Bishops. I and three other women deacons ordained in 1988 were all priested in 1990, Kathleen Young and Irene Templeton in the North in June, Janet Catterall in Cork in September and myself in Dublin in October.'

Daphne was involved with the Partners in Mission, working closely with Horace McKinley, both of them being the delegates to it from their diocese.

P.I.M. had grown out of a Congress on Mutual Responsibility and Interdependence held in Toronto in 1963. Daphne was interested in reaching out to both Christians and non-Christians, and in supporting and in collaborating with those of other faiths.

Like many others, Daphne was frequently distraught over violence in the North of Ireland. She would write out sentences and phrases to place around her study to remind her how it should be. From Gandhi 'Non violence is not a garment to be put on and off at will. Its seat is in the heart and it must be an inseparable part of our very being.' Another: 'There is no way to peace. Peace is the way. Peace is a process.' She composed prayers incorporating these notes.

Daphne wrote: 'I visited Australia in September 1992 and had dinner with a number of women from the Ministry of Women in Sydney. They were poised for their November Synod, at which the measure allowing ordination of women to the priesthood was to be passed by one vote.'

On November 19th, 2000, Canon Ginnie Kennerley preached a sermon in Christ Church Cathedral, Dublin, to mark the 25th anniversary of the commissioning of the first women Lay Readers in Dublin and Glendalough Diocese. To quote, in part:

At this service today, we are honouring five women of the Church of Ireland who twenty-five years ago made history by being commissioned to preach and lead worship in parishes of this diocese. Daphne Wormell, Patricia Hastings-Hardy, Audrey Smith, Thea Boyle and Joan Rufli became on November 16th, 1975, the first female Lay Readers, not in the Church of Ireland – for Clogher had jumped first – but in this diocese.

Dr Buchanan's commissioning of these five women as Lay Readers could hardly be seen as revolutionary in the context of the world-wide Anglican communion. But in the Irish context it was still remarkable. ... And only six months later the Archbishop was speaking eloquently in favour of the ordination of women to the priesthood ... to most of those present it was a novel idea. ...

Few of us could imagine what a woman minister might be like, and the possibility in the Church of Ireland seemed remote.

Or it did until we began to experience the ministry of these five women. They could not have been less like viragos. They were dignified, prayerful, intelligent, well able to expound scripture and to express themselves. They were distinctive in their pale blue scarves and magenta gowns. Certainly no one could have accused them of aping their male colleagues. But their presence in the sanctuary brought a new sense of completion and human balance to the conduct of worship. It is clear that the ministry of these five women, not only in the sanctuary but in committee rooms and synods, hospitals and schools, study groups and publications, was decisive for the relatively smooth progression of the church to the acceptance of women in the ordained ministry over the next fifteen years. ... It was important for the office of the reader in the church as well. ... May God's blessing rest on each one of our pioneers today; and may they know that the church affirms them, thanks them, and considers itself in their debt.

Jennifer Gill had taken over from Daphne with Ginnie Kennerley as co-chair of the Women's Ministry Group after the Synod's agreement to the ordination of women. The women coming into training from 1990 onwards seemed to assume that the battle had been won — and to a large extent it had. In January 2002, Jennifer wrote about Daphne: 'It was her great humanity that made her a very special person; loved by many but especially by those who came across her in the enormous contribution she made to women's ordination through the Women's Ministry Group. Had she been twenty years younger, Daphne would have been the first woman to be ordained.'

Revd Dr Michael Kennedy recently wrote: 'I look back on those years of struggle – which had their desolate moments, such as when the first women deacons' bill was ruled out of order – with a great sense of gratitude for the faithful band of those who kept the whole issue alive. Daphne was a wonderful "encourager" and very good at "networking." I think of Daphne, in the best possible sense, as a "people person", and this was the secret of her influence both in TCD and in the Church. Donald was such a strong supporter that he threatened to revert to Methodism if the legislation did not go through! I have such happy memories of them both.'

18

HOME TO CANADA 1964–2000, AND HOME...

The plane rumbled and swayed down the Dublin Airport runway, trying to gather enough speed to lift itself with all of us and all of our baggage into the air. We doubted whether the energy generated by the small engines would be sufficient. Possibly the trip, so crammed full with anticipation and excitement, would end up in a heap on one of the fields we had passed as we had driven towards the airport.

It was the morning of June 2, 1964. I was eighteen. I had just completed the Leaving Certificate examinations, so I had finished secondary school. The reward for early exam writing was the long, three-month summer holiday. I was being taken by Mum to visit Canada, the land of her birth, full of the places and the people of her childhood.

Mum was forty-eight. She had left home in 1937, twenty-seven years before, and this was her first return trip. Although she had always felt at home in Ireland, nevertheless she had suffered dreadfully from homesickness for Canada. Her youngest brother was twelve when she left; he was now thirty-nine, and married with four children. He would be meeting us in Toronto, with his whole family, and Mum worried that she would not be able to recognise anyone there. Many letters had been exchanged, describing clothes and colours and scarves and brooches that each party would be wearing.

Our flight was classified as a 'student flight' which meant for one hundred-and-thirty-two Irish pounds each, we could get to America. First stop was Shannon with a two-hour break for refuelling. Next, the plane took off for Gander, Newfoundland. More hours of waiting, further rattlings and shakings, and our third lift-off was achieved. We eventually made it to JFK Airport, in New York. We sorted out the passport checks and gathered our thirteen pieces of luggage. Mum had previously decided to utilise a porter to move all that baggage, and had inserted a folded American, five-dollar tip into her purse, a generous donation for those days. The porter was the largest man I had ever seen, and was the first black man who had ever spoken to me. I was mesmerised. 'Get out the tip from my purse,' Mum instructed me. 'It's in the special pocket.' I knew Mum had had to order the American money through her Irish bank, six months in advance. I handed him the carefully folded note. He snatched it from my hand, and disappeared into the milling crowd without a moment's pause. It was only later when we stopped for a bite to eat, and Mum told me we'd have to settle for a cup of tea, that I realised the tip I had put into that man's huge hand had been the one-hundred dollar bill she had also folded into the special pocket, in case of an emergency.

Following a tasty cup of tea and a four-hour wait, we were taking off again towards Toronto. The whole trip had been long and exhausting, and it was midnight by Irish time when we emerged into the bright sunlight and saw the fresh faces that greeted us in Toronto. It was the black and white photos that proved most helpful, for I recognised tall Uncle Brian, and Mum immediately spotted his wife. How often I have thought of each of those moments, as over the past thirty years I must have crossed the Atlantic about twice a year. That makes for over sixty crossings. Each lift-off jars my mind back to that first trip.

Today, jet engines are so powerful, larger suitcases are used and New York is by-passed. We can speed to Vancouver and refuelling stops are not required. We fly over Greenland and Hudson Bay. We slice across the Northwest Territories and head south over northern Alberta. Always reserving a window seat, I crane my neck into such a position that it feels like my head is actually sticking out of the window. What I'm watching for is the great Athabasca River, whose headwaters are formed by the Columbia Ice Field on the continental divide of the Rockies. This river winds and meanders north-eastward on a 1,231 kilometre trek, seeking Lake Athabasca, which is shared by Alberta and Saskatchewan. Finely ground particles of rock, or "rock flour", formed by glacial action, lend a silty grey colour to the water.

It is easy to spot the river from the air, but what I'm seeking particularly is a two-mile long island, nudging the eastern shore, 65 kilometres north of Fort McMurray. On June 1st, 1925, Daphne's father, a Dominion Land Surveyor based in Calgary, received a letter from Sidney Ells, an engineer with the Department of Mines in Ottawa. Today, Mr Ells is considered to be the father of research into methods of separating the oil from the sands in northern Alberta, initially to be utilised as a source of asphalt for the paving of roads that could open up the area. In fact, it was the Northern Alberta Railway line, completed in the 1920s, that gave developers the opportunity to pursue the Athabaska region's potential. The great prospects of the oil sands as a source of transportation fuel was only beginning to be realised.

In his letter, Mr Ells wrote:

June 1st, 1925

Dear Mr. Wallace,
With reference to my topographical maps of the Athabaska district, I find it is impossible to name a large lake in township 98 after your daughter since the Geographical Board considers it desirable to retain the old unofficial name.
I have, however, taken the liberty of naming a rather large Island in township 95, range 11, Daphne Island.
Trusting the above will meet with your approval, believe me,

Yours truly,
S. C. Ells

Daphne Island is named after our mother. In 1993, when she was 77, Mum and her sister Val set out to find Daphne Island. Journeying by car from Edmonton to Fort McMurray, and attempting to shortcut through the muskeg, several times they hit dead-end roads and had the front end of the car sinking into the bog. Eventually, Mum wrote in her diary, 'Incredible that we are really at Fort McMurray!' Next day, 21 August, they hired a captain and his small boat to motorboat down the Athabasca. The captain greeted them by saying he knew Daphne Island well. The river is wide, but there are many expansive, sandy shoals along its shoreline. These are not consistently on the same side of the river and must be navigated with great care, by switching from one side to the other. This manoeuvring doubles the mileage. Aided by black triangles to port, red triangles to starboard, the captain concentrated. 'I keep to the rules. That way, you don't get no surprises.'

Finally, the Island rose up six feet beside them, its top heavily wooded with aspen, poplar and birch. There was no beach and no obvious place to land, so they contented themselves with scrambling up the bank and pushing their way through the underbrush. They tried digging up some plants to take home but the ground was hard and unyielding and they hadn't brought any tools.

Several photos were taken of Daphne on her Island. In one, she is grasping a snapped-off birch twig, which she took as proof of landing. She pulled up an alder sapling which she brought to Vancouver Island, keeping the roots wrapped and moist. We optimistically planted it, but it didn't survive the winter. She was interviewed by the local newspaper, the *Fort McMurray Express*, and the edition published on August 30, 1993 had as front page headlines 'Namesake makes trip down memory lane.' Daphne is quoted: 'It was a really neat feeling to be on something named after me.' She had accidentally left her travel journal on the boat, but many months later it arrived through the letter-box in her house in Dublin.

Mum travelled to North America a number of times with Dad, and then, later, alone. Her final trip to Canada, in 2000, was to attend one of her grandchildren's university graduation ceremonies in eastern Canada. The direct flight to Toronto from Dublin was not long, but it was a great strain on her, physically. She was 84. She wrote: 'Looking old makes people kind to me. Young man escorted me through all the airport muddle.' At the Convocation she nobly clambered up the bleacher benches provided, and uncomplainingly sat out the long 3-hour wait on a hard bench, without a cushion. Of the ceremony she wrote: 'Bottom sore. Well organised.' Delighted and proud to be present, afterwards she sat in the big hall in a well-padded chair, watching the university colours and comradeship swirl around her. No doubt memories flooded through her mind. One of the dignitaries presiding was a professor from University College, Cork, and had she been younger she would have asked a few questions, and then have discovered she knew one of his relatives, or somehow had a personal connection.

I cried as I watched my son receive recognition, and I wept as I noticed my mother's growing frailty. The writing in her letters was now wobbling unevenly across the page. Mum was beginning to slip away from us.

It was during a visit to Dublin in the summer of 2001 that I summoned enough courage to ask Mum how she felt about dying. We were having dinner, and she paused, put down her knife and fork and forcefully said, 'What an amazing, exciting experience that will be!'

I was with her, holding her hand, as she died. We went to a place together, until I could go no further. She travelled on. It was 27th November, 2001.

My brother Stephen and his wife, Valerie came to the hospital. We took the brilliantly coloured freesias brought earlier by family friend, Sandra Ganly, and we strewed them across the snow white damask sheet that the nurses had laid out from her folded hands to the foot of the bed.

Fred Appelbe came to the bedside, and he now said prayers and verses from the Canadian Book of Common Prayer. He knew them well, telling us they were the best he had encountered.

But Mum had gone on her new purposeful adventure with her Donald, following her pilgrim way. It was time for her to cast aside her loneliness, her personal struggles, and to find new white trails to blaze across her sky.

In the Church of Ireland Review, January 2002, Fred Appelbe wrote, in part: 'Much has been written about Daphne in this review. For now, I will simply say that I loved and admired this woman without reserve and Christmas was painful and empty without her at the altar.'

Daphne's sister Dorothy wrote after Daphne's death, 'Daphne was rather special in my life. Being five years older she was always my tutor, my counsellor, my model in many ways… I depended on her wise advice about lots of things. When she went to Ireland I was 16 and I missed her dreadfully. I used to dream she was coming home.' Daphne's second sister Val, wrote: 'For each of us Daphne was a light in our development. We prospered under it. … She was a wonderful raconteur and to this day I remember the names and activities of some of her friends whom I never met. When she left home she left a void.'

The readings given at Daphne's funeral service were chosen by her. From the Meditations of John Donne:

The Church is catholic, universal, so are all her actions; all that she does belongs to all … God's hand is in every translation, and his hand shall bind up all our scattered leaves again, for that library where every book shall lie open to one another.

Another reading, 'Union of Friends' taken from 'Some Fruits of Solitude' by William Penn:

They that love beyond the World cannot be separated by it.
Death cannot kill, what never dies.

Nor can Spirits ever be divided that love and live in the same Divine
   Principle; the Root and Record of their friendship.

If Absence be not Death, neither is theirs.

Death is but Crossing the World, as Friends do the Seas; They live in one
   another still.

For they must needs be present, that love and live in that which is
   Omnipresent.

In this Divine Glass, they see Face to Face; and their Converse is Free, as
   well as Pure.

This is the Comfort of Friends, that though they may be said to Die, yet
   their Friendship and Society are, in the best Sense, ever present,
   because Immortal.

APPENDIX I

WOMEN AND THE CHURCH[10]

We live in an age of revolutionary violence when most established traditions are under attack, and we delude ourselves if we imagine that traditional Christianity is exempt from this challenge. It is not so much Christ and his message which are being criticized; there is still widespread acceptance of Christian values and in some quarters, notably in American universities, there is a revival of interest in theology. But there is growing impatience with the traditional forms in which Christianity expresses and organizes itself, and membership of the Christian church is no longer generally regarded as fundamental to a full life. Indeed in many circles to admit to being a church-going Christian is to stigmatize oneself as a limited personality. It is widely realized that the church has been driven underground in most communist countries; it is not so widely realized that there is a real possibility that Muslims are making more headway than Christians in Africa. The church is still far from accepting that the prevailing wind of agnosticism has changed the religious climate of the west from a high enthusiastic belief to a trough of disillusioned indifference. The response of a general in the field to this kind of thinning of the ranks and lowering of morale would be to call up his reserves. The reaction of the church is to continue to ignore one-half of its man-power, in other words its women.

[10] New Divinity: a Church of Ireland Journal Vol. 1 no. 2 November 1970 pages 32–41

As responsible adults we women do not welcome the difficulty of the church in its present critical situation as our opportunity. But many of us believe that the church's stature may well be further diminished by the continued denial of our desire to contribute to its life at a meaningful level. We are grateful to those who make it clear that we should be allowed to play a full part in the life of the church if we wish to do so, but we are also aware that there is entrenched opposition to any such suggestion. This article will try to argue that our opponents are moved not by reason but by prejudice, the same kind of prejudice as normally manifests itself whenever one section of the human race rationalizes its feeling of superiority over an underprivileged group.

Man's persistent inhumanity to women is one of the salient facts of history, running as it does through European tradition, which has always forced women to work harder for lower rewards and to have less scope (and less fun) than men. 'There is no subject on which the Christian church has always been (and in most cases still is) so retrograde, so subject to non-Christian, pagan notions of the sexes and to patriarchal thinking as in regard to women and their place in the church.'[11] Yet the germ of feminine emancipation is to be found in Christ's behaviour and attitude towards women, and it is widely supposed that Christianity differs from other religions in believing that women are equal to men. In the institutional church, however, some men have always been more equal than others and all men than women. We still are the second-class citizens of Christendom, and we are absolutely debarred from holding ordained office. There is an underlying attitude of hostility which is very wounding, and gives one a kinship with the feelings of others who are told they have been born inferior or subordinate. It is chastening to reflect that by condoning such discrimination the church finds itself, reluctantly one hopes, in the company of those who exploit subject peoples. There is also the unfortunate result that those who are discriminated against often end up tacitly accepting the situation. I think of the Negro who said to me 'If God had meant all men to be equal, he wouldn't have made them black and white, would he?' So also some of the most vociferous critics of feminine emancipation are to be found among women who perhaps mistrust the motives of those who desire to explore new fields because they themselves have no such impulse.

Like the black people of the southern states or the majority of the Irish for three hundred years, we are the church's kitchen staff and the minders of

11 Hendrik Kraemer, *A Theology of the Laity* (London, 1965), p. 69

children. 'Women in the church?' said one man to me. 'They make excellent cleaners.' We do not decry the need for the careful housework that makes for seemly worship, or under-estimate the feminine skills in beautifying the church with flowers and altar cloths. Of course there must be someone to type and tidy, and every administration needs a lower civil service to implement its decisions. But why in the church should the legislature and the executive be almost entirely male while women, often as highly qualified, are limited to typing other people's letters, making tea and acting as unpaid and unacknowledged curates? And how coyly we get talked down to!

Various reasons are put forward. First that we are weaker. We are glad enough to agree that most men are physically stronger than most women. We may also be less aggressive; we certainly don't yearn to be soldiers. But have we really less endurance and physical courage? One thinks of missionaries like Mrs. Livingstone and Gladys Aylward, 'The Small Woman.' We may have our little weeps, but these don't amount to as much as some men imagine, and may in fact give us strength to go on. Certainly we are no less ready than men to put up with discomfort. And mostly we live longer.

Perhaps it is argued that our brains are not as good as men's. The absence of intellectual giants among women is probably due chiefly to the difficulty women have in reconciling intellectual achievement with what our male-oriented society regards as the feminine role. 'Bluestocking' is still an insulting word. Indeed there is such a notably anti-intellectual attitude towards scholarship in some ecclesiastical quarters that one almost hesitates to mention that there are women genuinely interested in theology. Most of us are perhaps more intelligent than we let men know we are. I believe our minds are somewhat different from men's in that we find it more difficult to be theoretical, and we can fail to see the wood for the trees, particularly if the trees happen to be human. But we are interested in ideas, even if experience has taught us that it is usually prudent not to disagree openly with men. One of my aunts quoted her father as saying she had no right to think, and that she should do what a man told her; this attitude dies hard. If we speak up outside the family circle, men are inclined to wilt and label us as shrewish, or we are told more politely (by some members of the church for instance) that the world is too complex and harsh for us to become involved in it. I wonder if these people forget the circumstances of the Christ's birth, or that two women stood at the foot of the cross. My experience is that many women are eager to discuss and even get involved in the deeper problems of life, and that these problems should not be limited to children and home. The church does not seem to realize the need of most women for a stronger diet, nor measure up to the necessity of helping those who are groping for more mature attitudes to life.

Even if we have a reasonable chance of making the point that women are not physically or mentally inferior, we still have to remove the highest hurdle, the claim that we are emotionally unstable. Women, we are told, take things personally; we dwell on a slight when we should be moving on to larger considerations. In short, we get involved in situations with our feelings rather than with our minds. One is tempted to repeat the charge made earlier that emotional involvement with outmoded concepts is what is chiefly responsible for men's reluctance to let women become fully active members of the church. But to face the criticism squarely, I think it is true that we do at times fail to ignore slights, and imagine that we are being attacked personally when nothing of the kind was intended. But so do others who suffer from condescension and from being overlooked. And what of the social and psychological pressures of the kind which condone the weeping of little girls while boys are expected to be stoical? I suspect also that the emotional woman suffers from pent-up frustration. 'Resentment is the reverse side of dependence',[12] and tears and verbal explosions result when a woman has no other means of expressing herself adequately. 'Woman uses the "nervous crisis" to rebel against her subordination; this is her way of showing vestiges of power in a situation in which she is virtually powerless.'[13] I certainly have known women whose skill and aspirations have not found expression to become narrow-minded and self-centred and a prey to emotional forces of a neurotic kind. I have also known men to react to the same pressures in the same way.

Let me add quickly that the expression of emotion is not always a sign of neurosis. There is such a thing as genuine emotion, which is an uplifting force and which should be the stuff of religion. We must not underestimate the value of self-discipline, but I suspect that the Anglo-Saxon cult of the stiff upper lip has done the Anglican church a disservice. 'It seems to me that the pomposity of western religion, its tendency to fear the emotions and realities of personal life and try to take refuge in administrative achievement may have to do with its determined masculinity.'[14] As women know, the will is not always more

12 Simone de Beauvoir, *The Second Sex* (London, 1950), p. 576
13 Op. cit., p. 578
14 Monica Furlong, *With Love to the Church* (London, 1965), p. 93

186

important than feelings, and feminine influence in the higher echelons of the church might restore an emotional balance rather than upset it.

If what is keeping us out of the mainstream of church government is prejudice dressed up to look respectable, what lies behind this kind of prejudice? It may be the plain truth that many men so appreciate the luxury of having their creature comforts the chief concern of their wives that they fail to see that it is the Christian duty of every individual to rise to his *or her* full potential, and that this might mean that a wife should at times forego the pleasure of warming her husband's slippers in order to develop some of her own talents. It is noticeable that Christ very rarely criticized women, yet one of his few rebukes was for Martha, who was showing that very over-concern for domesticity which the church to my knowledge is not on record for condemning. The Gospel story highlights the comparison with Mary, who, we observe, is more interested in Christ's ideas than in looking after his physical needs.

There is no mention in the gospel of Martha and Mary having children and one cannot imagine that Christ would have taken the side of a woman who neglected her child to sit at his feet, unless the father was there to stand in for an hour or two, which in the Palestine of the day was most unlikely! It is a healthy sign that fathers are now sharing much more in the joy and responsibility of bringing up children, especially as it is becoming apparent from modern social research that their influence from the earliest age is more important than used to be realized. But if children gain from having both parents rocking their cradles this is not to deny that in our society the maternal influence is still the more important. In accepting this responsibility we should not reject the idea that many women need to express themselves in ways other than the caring for men and the mothering of children. Just as most men have realized long ago that their role in life is not restricted to being the protectors and feeders of women and children, so more and more women of our own day 'have a contract with life itself, an urge to creativeness which lies deeper than the maternal instinct.'[15] It is an unfortunate truth that women's work is never done – and what a barrier this is to our proper development![16] Even with modern conveniences it is very difficult to get any continuous free time if one takes one's duties as a home-maker seriously enough to allow for a margin of time for the extras of family life. We need all the help and encouragement we

[15] Laurens van der Post, *Venture to the Interior* (London, 1952), p. 10
[16] M. Ramelson, *The Petticoat Rebellion* (London, 1967), p. 25

can get to steer a course between over-conscientiousness on one hand, and the need to express ourselves on the other, but instead of active sympathy we hear undertones of disapproval from ecclesiastical corridors, as if by looking outwards we are somehow threatening the whole institution of marriage. This apparent inability to trust us is very upsetting. Take for instance the regulations that bar us from certain offices after we have married. These are an affront to our sense of duty. We have our own sensitive consciences, and I have yet to meet the committed Christian (and that is the group of women this article is mainly about) who will neglect her child even in the service of the church.

Many good and able women feel completely fulfilled at home, but others of us, whether from a feeling of isolation or because we wish to make use of early training, are restless, and we welcome the increasingly accepted pattern that there may be a place for us outside our homes when our children are less dependent. But not much of a place in the church! And how much more this affects the unmarried woman who might wish to do a challenging religious job, and finds herself instead caught in the net of unequal pay and blocked promotion. Even religious broadcasters and journalists reflect the obsession with women in the rôle of wives and mothers rather than as individuals. The church has shown itself a leader in the community effort to raise the status of itinerants, but still takes up its stand as an onlooker with a faint cheer from the sidelines where the emancipation of women is concerned. Is it asking too much to hope that the Church of Ireland has applied to give evidence to the Commission on the Status of Women which is now in session? Or is there any officer of the church who has been given sufficient responsibility to take such an initiative in this and other women's problems (such as desertion)? Above all the church should be putting its own house in order by letting women without delay have a proper share in its own councils and policy-making bodies. Why is its attitude so ambivalent? Do we lack spiritual qualities? Or can it be that men are afraid of us?

We don't need to hide in clocks to know that some clergy say, 'We can't have women taking over the church.' This statement is interesting. For one thing it has an ideological ring. There are undertones of hysteria in it, not based on reasoned fact but on emotional fears. It is almost as if we were being accused of being witches. The fear that if we are given a voice and some responsibility we shall misuse it is perhaps an expression of man's guilty conscience. After all he has for years exploited his womenfolk without fully realising it.[17] Men are unconsciously afraid that their livelihood and stature will be diminished by the emergence of a hitherto inferior order, much as poor whites fear competition from coloured people. They may conceal this feeling of male superiority by rationalizing it or burying it deep, but it is apt to erupt occasionally with startling force.

'Women to take over the church?' Isn't this also the language of big business – a take-over bid? But this concern with material domination and worldly power is completely alien to the spirit of Christianity, which speaks of service and ministry, of the lowest seats and of humility. I think it is also alien to the feminine ethos; to speak readily of power-structures tends to be a masculine preoccupation. Why should we want to take over? I hope there are leaders amongst us, but most of us do not pine for leadership, certainly not at the expense of a better man. It is true that there are a few shrill women's voices in the church, but the situation is not yet normal, and pioneers and lone rangers have to be tough to survive. Most of us deplore bossy women, and I believe we are capable of handling those amongst us who become unduly officious. We are not basically concerned with wielding power, but we do think we should be consulted when important decisions are being made. We do not wish to equate women with men as some of the more revolutionary groups seem to be advocating, but we are interested in the pooling of resources that results from the recognition that there is between the sexes an 'equality of difference' and a 'difference of equality.'[18] It is a step forward that there is at last one woman on the Standing Committee of the Church of Ireland General Synod and there have been outstanding contributions, though often as lone voices, from women on synods. But how much does this really amount to? This men's club reserves the best seats for men only! We are welcome to polish furniture and care for fabric, but what about major financial priorities? Life has trained us to make practical decisions and to value time in the making of them. This does not mean that the majority of women are automatically interested in office and committees, but there are also other ways in which women could use their talents for personal relationships and their abilities as catalysts and facilitators to help the church to be more in touch with what's going on. I can understand the reaction of the American Episcopalian woman who wants to be ordained when she said recently 'I'd like to tell bishops what it's all about. I'd like to be a pastor to bishops!'

[17] See *The Listener* (March, 1970) for an analysis of how medieval man feared as witches those women who had been wronged by society.
[18] de Beauvoir, op. cit., p. 686

No doubt such sentiments are shocking to many who lean heavily on the tradition that for two thousand years men have staffed the church. But the viewpoint cannot be overlooked. No doubt we fail to grasp some aspects of life which are obvious to men, but do they in turn realize how many of the matters they discuss at such length seem almost irrelevant to us, that 'the church so rarely seems to be arguing in our language about issues which seem to us to be important'?[19] Surely we should be striving to use all available insights in order to get a balanced perspective. But balance comes with equality. This is another way of saying that the time is fast approaching when women must be considered for ordination. Not only would an ordained woman be in touch with different aspects of life in and out of the church but she would also be the most likely person to get other women involved. Indeed unless there is something really worthwhile for her, and them, to do, and no spikes in the road to limit the journey, she is not likely to be there at all! There is a deep psychological need for women to know that they are accepted completely, just as the Irish in the United States grew in stature and were recognized by their fellow-countrymen as fully fledged Americans when John F. Kennedy became President. We women also need to be seen to be there. Many may never start if they know they won't be allowed to arrive.

A short article such as this is not the place to discuss the pros and cons of women in the ministry, but I should like to say that as it is now generally conceded that there is no theological barrier to the ordination of women; the burden of opposition lies with the traditionalists. Their strongest argument would seem to be that if it were proper for women to be ordained Christ would have numbered some among his twelve apostles. Have these critics ever considered the social implications of women wandering with a band of men round the hills of Galilee or in the streets of Jerusalem in A.D. 30?[20] There is a further point. 'The Twelve Apostles correspond to the new Israel. They were all Jews (although Jesus had found "greater faith than in all Israel" in the centurion in Capernaum), and they were all men. Jesus did not break away from Israel.'[21] The break took place at Pentecost with the sound of a mighty rushing wind. Women were then with Gentiles in the inner circle, but within a hundred years the social customs of the Gentile world took precedence over

19 Monica Furlong, p. 93
20 Christ had not included slaves or freedmen among his disciples. Is it suggested that this means he condoned slavery?
21 André Dumas, 'Biblical anthropology and the participation of women in the ministry of the church' in *Concerning the Ordination of Women* (Geneva, 1964), p. 34.

religious beliefs, and the church yielded gradually to the Graeco-Roman view that women's destiny should be fulfilled at home. Later the spread of the Muslim faith brought an even chillier wind, the effects of which have lasted into this century. May I suggest that one of the strengths of the Anglican church has been to acknowledge at times in its history that though tradition may be blowing along the accustomed way, the crosswind of the Spirit may be blowing even harder in another direction. Otherwise how could Canterbury ever have had the courage to break with Rome, or the insight to allow its clergy to marry if they wish?

I believe the church is facing another crisis of direction at the moment. I see its urgent immediate task to be the fostering of Christian community. All of us, men and women, need to gather together in a depth not reached in most parish worship so that we may scatter as more effective Christians. This should be familiar ground for the church: the building of *Koinonia* 'where there is neither Jew nor Greek, male nor female.' But you cannot proclaim community and practise exclusiveness. What is needed is the same spirit which inspired the actions of the second-class Jewish citizen when he allowed himself to be drawn into public discussion at the well with someone who was not only a Samaritan but also a woman. Women much appreciate the help of those who are following in his footsteps and taking up our cause with vision and courage. There are indeed signs that the countryside is opening up before us; perhaps along one of the new highways bishops may yet be bringing their husbands to Lambeth.

Daphne Wormell

APPENDIX II

ELIZABETH MOLONEY FORMER PRESIDENT OF THE IRISH PRE-SCHOOL PLAYGROUPS ASSOCIATION

I had already just started a small playgroup, and there were about ten others who also had groups. We thought we could start up an Irish Playgroups Association similar to one that had been set up in England, but we didn't know how to go about setting up an Association. How should we do it? What were the steps we needed to take? What were the legal requirements and the Government's requirements? What was our ethos? Did we need memoranda about setting up Playgroups? I was determined to get an Association organised and to build it on a good footing.

I met Daphne and told her about this, and she said to me, 'You can do it, and I'll come along with you.' She was a marvellous person who opened up a whole world to me. She worked especially with Molly Walmsley and Maureen Hope. We set up a Committee in 1969, and we held a number of meetings among ourselves. We were full of enthusiasm. Daphne and Molly Walmsley would say they would stay for the business part of the meeting only and then they'd go off home, and the rest of us would stay on for hours, sometimes to 5:30 a.m., working out what we needed to do with the children.

Daphne calmly and firmly knew where she was going with the Playgroups, how to set it all up and she always felt she was going to achieve that objective. And she didn't get upset by other people's objections and obstacles.

For example, it was through her encouragement and determination that a training group for playgroup leaders was to start in the evenings. It was to be held in Ballyfermot. We went out there to join up for the course, and it was shut down that very night. Father McQuaid, the Roman Catholic Archbishop, stopped it. He was of the 'older school' and he felt we were taking the children away from their mothers. Most of us, the ten leaders, and some others were stunned, really devastated. Archbishop McQuaid explained to me that the parents might start 'gossiping' among themselves, a most dangerous occupation, and that he had no choice but to cancel the training courses.

We set out to educate the Government on the importance of playgroups. The ten or so of us went in to see the Minister for Education and his civil servants. But we failed in persuading them about the importance of playgroups. The Minister asked me, 'What will the children's mothers be doing when their young children are at playgroups?' I replied, 'It will be only from 9 to 11:45 in the morning. There is not much they *can* do in such a short time.' But we got nowhere.

However, Daphne persevered. She moved in what she called 'baby steps' without any racket, and slowly she managed to change things.

We began to give radio interviews. We applied for a grant from the Government, and to businesses, like Easons, for equipment. Everyone was fantastic – the grant came through and the shops let us take 'anything we wanted.' The Lego company sent ten crates of Lego in a huge lorry, which pulled up in the street in front of my house. With this money and this equipment we planned to go around the country giving demonstrations. We would contact a community and we would be given a hall, or a room in a school. Once, even the Jesuits gave us a place. We would take our equipment to the venue, set it all up and throw open the doors. Children and parents would come in and all played together, down there on the floor. Sometimes men came in alone and played on the floor with the push-around trains. They would get lost in the playing and they would start to say, 'Choo-Choo! Choo-Choo!'

All of the husbands were wonderfully understanding. Donald would be there, enjoying it all. In fact, all the husbands eventually joined us, having heard all our talk and having listened to the radio interviews we had been giving. And all day at these demonstrations I'd be there, talking to Daphne.

She supported us all in everything we tried to accomplish.

We all felt that children learn through their play. Play is how they find out about themselves and everything around them. Daphne was keen on children discovering themselves, and she said they should be like entrepreneurs, trying new things. She insisted the word 'play' be kept in 'playgroups', even when the Department of Education was finally becoming involved and attempted to alter the title to Early Childhood Education.

Daphne also believed parents should be involved with their child in this exploration; not in a 'showing' capacity, but rather by exposing the child to experiences. And while this discovery process was in action, a child should not be interrupted, if possible, but given time and space for play. Daphne would say, 'A child's play is a child's work, and it should be respected as such. This is where and how a child learns to concentrate, and he or she should be allowed to do so without interruptions.'

Daphne was keen on the education side of training for the Playgroup leaders. Eventually, we *were* able to put on 10-week courses for Playgroup leaders, which were offered at first one night each week. When we were developing the courses, I remember asking Daphne, 'Who's going to tutor these courses?' She replied, 'You.' I exclaimed, 'Oh, no!' Daphne continued, 'You and the other Playgroup leaders are the people who know why playgroups are important to children and their parents, and you know what should happen in the playgroups. So you are the people that should be the tutors.' And so she persuaded me, and I co-tutored the sessions. About 24 mothers attended the courses and all wanted to start their own playgroups. We called ourselves the IPPA. – the Irish Pre-School Playgroups Association.

At these sessions Daphne wanted us to emphasize that groups should be fun, and games should be played by the children. She told us if children do things with their hands they will learn and remember. She explained if children act out events, whether historical like a princess's wedding or the Olympics, or current as in going shopping or driving a bus, these children would remember what they learned. And in spiritual development and in moral development the playgroup leaders would be models for the children. She would say, 'The children take their lead from you.' For example, during playgroups there would be no need for any shouting, no child would be upset by adults around him or her, and so the children would learn to be respected and to show respect for each other.

The women that took those courses still say to me, 'Do you remember that

WITH DIGNITY AND GRACE

lovely, gentle woman?' Daphne and I had such a nice friendship, built by her. I'll always regard her as my friend. I was about 20 years younger than she was, but this made no difference to her. Daphne had a wealth of experience behind her, but she never said 'I know how it should be because I know more.' She, and Molly too, were not that much older than us, but they were far wiser than we were.

Daphne helped me in another way. One of my sons took O-Level exams in a gap year. When the results came in, the counsellor-priest told me my son should go to work behind the counter in the Bank. I happened to show the results to Daphne, and she suggested I put him forward instead as a candidate for Entrance Scholarship at Trinity. So I began the process of applying, but I had to have the Entrance application form signed by someone at my son's school. They flatly refused. On hearing this, Daphne said, 'I'll sign it.' So she did, taking great pleasure in helping me. The form went in, my son wrote the exams and he was awarded an Entrance Scholarship. He now has 11 degrees, including a doctorate, and he loves academia. To think all of that might have been lost to him! I was so grateful to Daphne. When the results were announced the priests celebrated my son's achievements, gathering the whole school together, and since that time they have encouraged other boys to apply for Scholarship.

Daphne was a very patient, spiritual person. In her later years she had a good friend Father Simeon, who was a spiritual advisor, a priest, in a hospital. It was wonderful for so many people to see a priest show such respect for a woman, like Father Simeon[22] did for Daphne. She was breaking down the traditions in another church, and he opened up to her and accepted her as an equal. They both got very excited during their discussions. You could see Daphne was fantastic with all types of men and women from all walks of life.

The IPPA went on, and we did eventually get money from the Government to have an official advisor. It was a Fine Gael Government who gave us that money, but when they were replaced by a Fianna Fáil Government the money was taken away. We had spent a long time looking for that money, and the Fianna Fáil politicians had promised to maintain our funding of 1.5 million pounds, a considerable sum for back then. After that election I met one of those politicians in Dunne's Shopping Centre. I challenged him about the

---

22 Daphne met Father Simeon 'by a fluke.' He had needed a phone, and he just happened to ring Daphne's doorbell to ask for the use of hers. They got talking, and from then on they were very good friends.

withdrawing of our grant, and he told me, 'What politician keeps promises after an election?' So I went on the radio many times about that. I told that politician 'I'm going to march' but privately I worried I'd be doing so alone. However, many joined with us. We threatened a sit-in, the Government capitulated and they gave us the money again. What a waste of time and air-space!

Two further issues rose up, one being the Government's idea that 4-year-old children should be sitting in desks all day, not 'playing.' We went to Fianna Fáil headquarters, objecting, and made our point that play and education were the same for 4-year-olds. Another issue we tackled was the prevention of slapping of children in schools. We made numerous submissions on the problem to the Government, and we were in the Dáil, day in and day out. Eventually they changed the law about slapping in school, and we attended the Dáil for that occasion.

Elizabeth Moloney

The description above was given by Elizabeth Moloney when we met on September 7, 2008. She said, 'I will make you a cup of tea, like all those times when Daphne would come here to discuss something with me. We would talk a long time over a good cup of tea.'

Elizabeth's parents had come to Dublin from Macroom, Co. Cork. She was born, one of seven, in Clontarf, Dublin. The children were sent to a private pre-school, Elizabeth going when she was two-and-a-half, keeping company with her sister who was one year older. On completing preschool, the children had a Governess until Elizabeth was nine years old. Elizabeth declared, 'So you can see I was not going to be bossed around by teachers.' When Elizabeth had children of her own she had a room built onto the house at the back, and she opened a preschool for her own children.

Today, the IPPA is flourishing, and puts out a magazine called 'Children@Play.' Underneath this title on the front cover is written: 'Magazine of IPPA, the Early Childhood Organisation. IPPA – Playgroups and Daycare.' The IPPA values listed inside are:

The human rights of children
All children equally
The uniqueness of each child
Childhood
Play

The primacy of families in the lives of children
All adults who support children and families
The communities in which the child and family are embedded.

The ideals of those who set up this Association are still prominent, shining through to the benefit of all those Irish children who have attended, are attending and will attend Playgroups and Daycare.

Julia Turner
September 2008

INDEX

A

Aberhart, William, 34
Appelbe, Rev Fred, 132, 155, 181
Arnold, D. O., Principal Nepean High School, 17, 20
Aspley Guise, England, 84
Auburn House near Malahide, 41

B

Bacon, Francis, 160
Bailey, Kenneth, 65
Balrath House, near Kells, 46
Benson, Charles, 152
Blessington, 131
Bowness, near Calgary, 3, 5, 13, 20, 31, 32, 33, 47
Boydell, Dr Brian, 102
Boydell, Mary, 102
Boyle, Thea, 108, 109, 175
Bradwell, England, 77
Brownstown House, 37–48, 62
Buchanan, Archbishop Alan, 87, 158, 171
Buchanan, Mrs, 161
Budd, Ann, 152
Burrows, Canon Walter, 155, 162

C

Caird, Archbishop Donald, 110
Calgary, 3–20, 31, 33, 37, 38, 43, 49–54, 73, 113, 114, 130, 139, 140, 153, 179
    Army Corps, 83
    Crescent Heights High School, 33, 34
    Mount Royal College, 35
Church of Ireland Board of Education, 145
Church of Ireland Magazine, The, 146
Coady, Jack, wedding photographer, 73
Cole, Betty. *See* Harman, Betty
Cooper, Edith, 73
Courtenay, Ted, 119
Craig, Joyce, 66, 96, 149, 151
Crozier, Archdeacon, 58
Cunningham, Miss E. M., 44, 64, 68
Curtis, Prof Edmund, 67, 70

D

de Brún, Pádraig, Monsignor, 70
Deverell, William, 110
Dillon, Rev John Jeffcott, 155
Donne, John, Meditations, 181
Dowrick, Cherry, 127, 133, 134
Dowrick, Frank, 133
Dublin University Women Graduates Association (DUWGA), 149
Duggan, Bishop Jack, 91, 110

E
Elizabethan Society, 62, 67
Engineering School, TCD, 44

F
Faris, Phyllis, 110
Fassett, Quebec, 18–24
Fitzwilliam Street, Lower, No. 15, 42
Fosbery, Harry, 17
Fosbery, Helen, 17, 20–26
Friends of the Library, 151
Fry, Matty, Senior Lecturer TCD, 57
Furlong, Prof Ned, 73, 115

G
Ganly, Sandra, 181
Gilbert, Margaret, 110
Gill, Jennifer, 110, 176
Godfrey, Mr, 60
Godfrey, Mrs, 56
Goligher, Vice-Provost TCD, 63, 96,
    134
Greer, Leslie, (née Tyrrell), 61, 96, 153
Griffith, Miss, 60
Gwynn, Katherine, 145
Gwynn, Rose, 96, 141

H
Harman, Betty, 63, 68, 72, 99, 115, 162
Hastings-Hardy, Patricia, 104, 108,
    109, 162, 169, 170, 175
History Society, 66, 67
Hope, Maureen, 193
Hudson's Bay Company, 51
Hutton, John, 60

I
Irish Housewife, The, 142, 144
Irish Housewives Association, 142, 144
Irish Pre-School Playgroups Assoc, 135
    AGM 1973, 148
Irish Times, The, 146

J
Jordan, Maria, 64

K
Kearon, Rev Kenneth, 167
Keating, Jim, 133
Keating, Kitty, 100, 133
Keating, Sarah, 133
Kelso, Norah, 151
Kennedy, Rev Dr Michael, 164, 176
Kennerley, Ginnie, ix, x, xii, 109,
    167–176
    25th anniversary Dublin women lay
        readers, 175
Kentstown, near Navan, 38
Kilkee, 131
Knockmark House, 43
Knockrabo School, 144

L
Larmour, Nancy, 83
Layton, Turner, 141
Ledbetter, Peter, 155
Lennon family, Co. Meath, 17
Leverett and Frye, 57
Liddle, Katherine, née Gwynn, 145
Luce, Frank, 110, 165
Luce, John, 108, 152
Luce, Lyndall, 108

M
Marshall, Rev William, 110, 155
McClatchey, Diana, 166, 167, 174
McConnell, A.J., Provost
    Government grant for TCD, 70
McGilligan, Joyce. See Craig, Joyce
McKinley, Rev Horace, 162, 164, 169,
    174
McQuaid, Archbishop John Charles,
    194
Meath Hospital, 42
Micks, Dr Robbie, 68
Micks, Fanny, 68

Milne, Dr Kenneth, 146
Mitchell, Dr David, 90
Mitchell, Dr Tom, Provost TCD, 108, 119
Moloney, Elizabeth, 148
Monsignor Paddy Brown. *See* de Brún, Pádraig
Montreal, 11, 18, 19, 37
Moody, Dr Theo, 56, 70
    Daphne postgraduate student, 113
    Daphne's wedding, 73
    Fellow TCD, 69
Moody, Margaret, 73
Murphy, Aunt Amos, 41, 154
Murphy, Aunt Bessie, 88, 89
Murphy, Aunt Geraldine, 64
Murphy, Aunt Maureen, 70
Murphy, Aunt Olive, 12, 36–41, 46, 48, 49, 62, 71, 72
Murphy, Aunt Vera, 63, 72, 96, 134, 140
Murphy, Edward, 99
Murphy, Eva. *See* Wallace, Eva
Murphy, Grandmother Emmeline Annie (*née* Lennon) 12, 13, 42, 55, 57, 58, 59
Murphy, Uncle Charlie, 38, 41, 44, 67, 73, 115, 154
Murphy, Uncle Cyril, 42, 49, 57, 59, 62–68, 72, 73, 96, 114
    Daphne as postgraduate, 70
    Daphne as Trinity student, 55
    Daphne's wedding, 73
    offer to pay fees at TCD, 53
Murphy, Uncle Leo, 96

N
Napier, Bella, Nannie, 109, 133–135
Nesbitt, Evelyn, 96
New Bradwell, England, 77, 82
Norman, Harold, 65
Norris, Senator David, 151

O
Ottawa
    Golden Street, Highland Park, 15
    House of Commons, 16

P
Park House School, 130, 144
Parke, Anstice, 72, 73, 97, 99, 115
Parke, Herbert, 72, 135
Parke, Nan, 72, 73, 97
Paterson, Dean John, 109
Penn, William, Union of Friends, 181
Perrin, Archdeacon Donald, 110
Phillips, Prof Alison, 56, 66–69
Pilkington, Clarissa, 149
Princeton, Institute for Advanced Study, 151

R
Rathcore Rectory, 59
Rathmichael Parish, 110, 153, 155
Roberts Café, 49
Ross, Charles, Aunt Olive's husband, 36
Roundstone, 132
RTE Outlook, 146, 162
Rufli, Joan, 108, 109, 175
Runcie, Archbishop Robert, 166
Russell, Mr, Bursar, TCD, 49, 57

S
Sagarra, Eda, 151
Shaw, Captain, Senior Lecturer's Office TCD, 56
Skibbereen, 132
Skryne Castle, 40
Smith, Audrey, 108, 109, 175
St Ann's, Dawson St., 42, 65
St Brigid's Society, 165
Stanford, Prof W. B., 61, 71

T
Tamplin, Hazel, 174
Tara, Hill of, open air service, 45

TCD Association and Trust, 151, 154
Thrift, Harry, 60
  tutor to Daphne, 56
Thrift, W. E., Provost, 61, 69
Tobias, Helen, 96
Toronto, 5, 8, 17, 175–180
Trinity College Races, 44
Trinity Hall, 44, 63–67, 145
Tyrrell, Leslie. See Greer, Leslie

W
Waddell, Ginete, 96
Wallace, Anna Maria (née Dillon), 155
Wallace, Aunt Jane, 7, 11, 22, 25, 86, 87
Wallace, Brian, 94, 95
Wallace, Daphne, See Wormell,
  Daphne
Wallace, Dorothy, 95, 181
Wallace, Eva (née Murphy), 94, 95, 139
  birth of Dorothy, 7
  birth of Hugh, 7
  Dublin 1924 with 4 children, 11
  making butter, 33
  visit to Dublin 1946/47, 90
  visit to Ireland 1936, 53
Wallace, Hugh, 94, 95
Wallace, James, 95
  Calgary, back from Ottawa, 20
  graduation, TCD, 1892, xiv
  marriage to Eva Murphy 1915, xiv
  move to Ottawa, 1925, 15
Wallace, Val, 90, 94, 95, 121
Walmsley, Molly, 148, 193
Watts, Mortimer, 35
Webb, Melissa (née Stanford), 154
Werner, Tony, 71
Williams, Brian, 126
Wilson, David, Dean St Patrick's, 64
Wilson, Doris, 63, 72, 99
Wilson, Dr, 90
Wilson, Prof R.G.A., 125
Women's Ministry Conference TCD
  1986, 167

Women's Ministry Group, ix, 110, 165,
  166, 174, 176
Wormell, Daphne
  aged about 2 years, 93
  Alexandra College teacher, 145
  birth 1916, 3
  birth of Julia, 130
  birth of Richard, 81
  birth of Robin, 131
  birth of Stephen, 131
  Bletchley Park, 77
  Board of Education of Church of
    Ireland, 145
  Calgary to TCD 1937, 54
  Canada, return after 27 years, 177
  Child of the Depression, 143
  Christ Church Cathedral, Waterford,
    address, 159
  Daphne Island
    photo, 107
    visit, 179
  death, 181
  depression, 133
  Dublin, return 1944, 88
  DUWGA, President, 149
  Family Reunion, 153
  father's rules, 140
  first dance with Donald, 71
  funeral service, 181
  Gatineau purchase, 91
  Glenstall 1987 address, 171
  Gold Medal, 113
  hair loss, 141
  High School teacher, 158
  Hillcourt teacher, 144
  history, selection of course, 56
  honeymoon, 74
  Honorary MA, 152
  house organisation, 137
  Hudson's Bay Company Calgary,
    working at, 51
  Irish Housewife, The, 142

Irish Pre-School Playgroups
    Association, Chairperson, 135
Irish Times, The, 146
Knockrabo School teacher, 144
lay reader 1975, 157
lay reader robes, 160
letter writing, 153
Librarian History Library, 66
marriage proposal from Donald, 71
Ministry of Women Conference,
    Canterbury 1986, 169
Ministry of Women in Sydney 1992,
    175
Mod, working for, 68
mother's visit 1946/47, 90
Mount Royal College, Calgary, 35
on Dublin, 140
paper on women's ordination with
    Rev Dr Kennedy, 1979, 165
parenting, 129, 147
Park House teacher, 144
Photo Calgary 1936, 95
playgroups, 148, 193
pregnancy in Cambridge, 76
Princeton for Don's sabbatical, 151
Religious Education of the Child, 159
RTE Outlook, 146
Scholar on same day Donald a Fellow
    TCD, 69
Scholarship announced 1939, 62
Scholarship urged by Mr Godfrey, 61
Senior Freshman, 56
sermons, 163
sister Val arrival at TCD, 90
Skerries 1924, 93
St Hilda's School for Girls, 8
starts as Senior Freshman, TCD, 35
student tutor to chidren, 65
teenage photos 1930 & 1932, 94
teenage tasks in Canada, 140
tour guide, 145
Trinity Book Sale, 151, 152
Trinity Hall, 63

wedding group 1941, 99
wedding photo, 98
wedding to Donald, 73
Women in the Church, 157
Women's Ministry Conference TCD
    1986, address, 167
Women's Ministry Group, 166
Wormell, Donald, 70–73, 81, 97,
    113–126, 154, 158, 169–176, 181,
    194, 204
    wedding group 1941, 99
    Bletchley Park
        appointment 1942, 76
        code breaking, 79
        Dambusters, code breaking, 79
        D-Day landings, code breaking, 79
        start 1942, 77
    Fellow TCD on day Daphne a
        Scholar, 69
    first dance with Daphne, 71
    honeymoon, 74
    Junior Proctor Dublin University, 70
    marriage proposal to Daphne, 71
    parenting, 129
    Perse School, 116
    Public Orator, Dublin University,
        152
    Royal College of Surgeons, 120
    Rouse, Dr W.H.D., teacher, 116–117
    TCD, Prof Latin 1942, 117
    TCD, return to, October 1944, 87
    Yale PhD, 117
    wedding photo, 98
    wedding to Daphne, 73
Wormell, Florence, 116
Wormell, Joanna, 125
Wormell, Julia, 99, 109
Wormell, Richard, 99, 100
Wormell, Robin, 100
Wormell, Stephen, 100, 181
Wormell, Thomas, 116
Wormell, Thomas Wilson, 116
Wormell, Valerie, 181